A TASTE OF

PARK CITY

PAST & PRESENT

Published by

1912 Sidewinder, Suite 201
Park City, UT 84060
800-438-6074

Library of Congress Cataloging-in-Publication Data: 96-078067

A TASTE OF
PARK CITY
PAST & PRESENT

PARK CITY
EDUCATION FOUNDATION

The Park City Education Foundation is a non-profit tax-exempt organization whose purpose is to raise funds and provide resources to enhance the education of students in the Park City, Utah school district. Proceeds from the sale of this cookbook will be placed in the endowment fund which provides funding for educational grants.

ACKNOWLEDGEMENTS

Park City Education Cookbook Committee

Peg Anderson/Co-Chairman
Carla Coonradt/Co-Chairman
Connie Sutterfield
Teresa Woodard
Priscilla Watts

Assistants

Kristine Anderson
Pat Boldt
Hal Compton
Sandra Hall
Nancy Langford
Claire Pierre
Carole Sanders
Kitty Stothart

Book Design

Green Design & Advertising, Inc.
Catherine Green

Production Coordinator
Keith Monson

Photography Courtesy of

The Main Street Photographer,
Nick Nass Collection

Park City Chamber Bureau,
Lori Adamski-Peek

Park City Historical Society & Museum,
Glenn Peterson Collection

TABLE OF CONTENTS

INTRODUCTION

In 1868, three soldiers stationed at Camp Douglas in Salt Lake City traveled over the summit from Big Cottonwood Canyon to what is now known as Park City. They were prospecting for gold and silver and discovered a rich outcropping of silver-bearing ore. Their stake would become Flagstaff mine, the beginning of a successful mining era for the city. News traveled fast, and soon, other prospectors arrived to stake their claims. The first settlement was known as Lake Flat located where Deer Valley's Silver Lake Village is today. There was a crystal clear alpine lake there called Silver Lake, and the miners built their little houses on its shores. Cold winter weather drove the miners to resettle at lower elevation, where Main Street is today. This was a good thing because later, Silver Lake was accidentally depleted of its water due to a mine drain tunnel.

By July 4, 1872 a mining town had emerged, and its renaming was put to vote. Parley's Park City won the toss, named in honor of early Mormon settler Parley P. Pratt. Soon after, the word Parley's was dropped from the name entirely. By 1881, Park City was the third Utah town to have telephone service and one of the first cities to have electric lights. By this time, the population had exploded to over 5,000. The mining business was thriving. In fact, the Hearst family fortune originated in Park City with the purchase of the Ontario mine.

The October 25, 1879 edition of the Salt Lake Tribune reported, "The town of Park City is rapidly approaching the size and appearance of a healthy, compact and permanent place. Town lots are selling readily, and commanding a very flattering figure. Lots that two years ago sold for $10 to $20 are now bringing from $100 up."

After weathering the boom and bust of mining, the tragedy of fire, the rebirth of the city and the growth of the ski industry, Park City is here to stay. Today, while mining has been put on hold, Park City is best known as Utah's popular ski and summer resort enhanced by the variety of people that have made this place their home. This wonderful place called Park City is a varied menu of **past and present**.

RESTAURANTS

Daly Mine Dining Room

*Dining rooms have always been a highlight of Park
City. During mining times rules were the
order of the day: "Sociability and good fellowship is
encouraged, but loud and boisterous talking,
vulgarity or profanity will not be permitted in the
dining room."*

(Silver King Bunk House Rules)

Salmon Crusted in Horseradish, Garlic and Herbs
Serves 2

2 steak cut salmon (12 oz. each) with skin on and deboned

Crust:
2 cups shallots, chopped fine
6 garlic cloves, chopped fine
2 oz. horseradish
1/2 cup mayonnaise
1/2 oz. fresh dill, chopped
salt and pepper to taste

Sauce:
2 shallots, chopped fine
1 cup sherry wine vinegar
1 cup cream
10 oz. butter

Mise en Place:
3 Roma tomatoes, diced
1 cup spinach, blanched
8 oz. fresh fettuccine
3 garlic cloves, slices
1 cup wild mushrooms, sliced

Combine crust ingredients. Set aside. For sauce: Sauté shallots. Add vinegar and reduce to one-third. Add cream. Let reduce to one-half. Cut butter into mixture very slowly with a whisk. Do not overheat. Sear salmon. Top with crust and bake until firm to the touch. While salmon is baking, cook pasta and sauté mushrooms, spinach and tomatoes. Remove skin off salmon. Place in nest of pasta and vegetables. Cover with sauce.

Chicken and Tortilla Soup
Serves 4

Broth:
1/4 small white onion, diced
2 cloves garlic, sliced
olive oil
1/4 teaspoon ground cumin
1 tomato, peeled, seeded and diced
2 1/2 cups chicken broth
1/2 cup enchilada sauce
1 small can diced green chiles
salt and pepper

Garnish:
4 tortillas, cut into strips and fried until crisp
1 avocado, diced
6 oz. cooked, shredded chicken breast
4 oz. Monterey Jack cheese, grated
cilantro leaves

To make broth, sauté onion and garlic in a little olive oil. Add the cumin, tomato, chicken broth, enchilada sauce and diced green chiles. Bring to a boil, then puree, a little at a time, in a blender (be careful). Return to heat, bring to a simmer and season with salt and pepper. Pour the broth into four bowls and garnish with tortilla strips, diced avocado, shredded chicken, grated cheese and cilantro leaves.

Grilled Sea Bass Salad with Raspberry Vinaigrette
Serves 4

4   4 oz. sea bass fillets
oil
salt and pepper
1/2 lb. mixed fresh baby greens
20 blanched asparagus spears
1/2 cup red onion, thinly sliced
1/2 pint fresh raspberries
1/4 cup thinly sliced fresh chives
lemon wedges (garnish)

Raspberry Vinaigrette:
1/4 cup water
1/2 cup raspberry vinegar
1 cup good quality salad oil
1/2 tablespoon Dijon mustard
1/2 pint fresh raspberries
salt and pepper
pinch of sugar

Raspberry Vinaigrette: Place all ingredients except oil in food processor and blend. While machine is running, slowly add oil in a steady stream until incorporated. Brush sea bass fillets with oil and season with salt and pepper. Place on hot grill and cook for 3-4 minutes on each side or until done. Toss baby greens with red onion and divide on four chilled plates. Arrange 5 asparagus spears on each plate and sprinkle with fresh raspberries. Gently set sea bass on top of greens. Drizzle entire salad with raspberry vinaigrette. Sprinkle with chives and garnish with lemon wedges.

Polenta Soufflé with Forest Mushrooms Ragout

Serves 6-8

2 cups water
1/2 cup polenta (dried)
3/4 cup good quality grated Parmesan cheese
salt and white pepper to taste
pinch of nutmeg
3 eggs, separated
6-8   2 1/2 oz. soufflé ramekins, buttered and floured

Mushroom Ragout:
1/4 lb. thin sliced pancetta, cooked until crisp, reserve 1 tablespoon fat
1/4 cup good quality virgin olive oil, divided
2 lb. assorted wild and cultivated mushrooms (porcini, chantrelle, shitake, morel, etc.)
1/2 teaspoon chopped garlic
1 teaspoon minced shallot
1/2 cup white wine (optional)
3 cups chicken stock
1 cup carrots, diced 1/4" thick
1 cup blanched and peeled pearl onions
1/2 teaspoon chopped fresh sage
1/2 teaspoon chopped fresh parsley
teaspoon lemon juice

For polenta: Bring water to a boil in a heavy saucepan and stir in polenta. Reduce heat and stir over low heat scraping bottom and sides of pan for approximately 30-40 minutes. Remove from heat and let cool slightly. Stir in Parmesan and seasonings. Let cool to room temperature. Add egg yolks to polenta and stir until smooth. Whip egg whites at room temperature until whites form firm peaks. Fold whites into polenta and spoon into soufflé ramekins to the top of the rim. Bake on a sheet pan, at 450 degrees, for approximately 15-20 minutes.

For mushroom ragout: In a large sauté pan, sauté pancetta until crisp. Drain on a paper towel and reserve 1 tablespoon of removed fat. Combine reserved fat and 2 tablespoons of olive oil. Add mushrooms to warm oil and sauté for a couple of minutes. Add garlic, shallots, wine and stock. Simmer, covered, for 5 minutes or until mushrooms are tender. Remove lid, add carrots and onions. Reduce liquid. Add crumbled pancetta, herbs, 2 tablespoons of olive oil and lemon juice. Serve ragout in decorative bowls. Invert polenta soufflé molds onto ragout and enjoy.

AT DEER VALLEY

McHenry's
Grilled Chicken Quesadillas
Serves 6

3 6 oz. boneless chicken breasts,
  skin on
12 6-inch flour or whole wheat tortillas
1 Anaheim chili, large
1 red bell pepper
1 red onion
1 tablespoon whole butter
12 oz. Jack cheese, grated
12 oz. Cheddar cheese, grated
  (mix both cheeses together)
2 teaspoons ground cumin
2 teaspoons chili powder
2 teaspoons garlic powder
2 teaspoons onion powder
1 tablespoon salt
1 tablespoon black pepper

sour cream (garnish)
fresh salsa (garnish)

Mix the last six seasonings together in a small bowl. Place chicken breasts on hot grill, skin side down. Dust breasts liberally with seasoning mixture. When skin is well browned and crisp, turn breasts, dust again and cook until done. Set cooked breasts aside to cool. Fine dice the chili, red bell pepper and onion. Place a sauté pan on high heat and add butter. When butter bubbles and begins to brown, add the diced vegetables and cook 2-3 minutes until just tender. Transfer from pan to a large mixing bowl and let cool. Remove skin from chicken breasts, slice lengthwise in half, then thinly slice widthwise the entire breast.

Add sliced meat to vegetables in mixing bowl. Add half the Jack and cheddar cheeses and remaining seasoning dust to meat and vegetables and mix all together very well. Set out six tortillas on work surface and distribute 1/2 of the remaining cheese onto each tortilla. Evenly distribute the chicken mixture atop the cheese, then top each with the remaining grated cheese and cap each with remaining tortillas, pressing tortilla firmly onto filling. Preheat sauté pan (or griddle) on medium heat (375 degrees) and cook quesadillas on dry surface until tortilla is browned and cheese melts (approximately three minutes per side). Cut each cooked quesadilla into six equal wedges and place on serving plates. Top each wedge with a circle of sour cream, and fill each sour cream circle with a small portion of fresh salsa.

Thai Coriander Chicken Wings
Serves 6-8

2 lb. chicken wings, cut into sections
1/2 teaspoon fresh garlic, chopped fine
1/4 teaspoon crushed red pepper
1 cup white sugar
1 cup soy sauce
1 cup cornstarch
1/4 cup whole coriander seed, crushed
1/8 cup sesame oil

Heat sesame oil in saucepan until it begins to smoke. Add crushed red pepper and garlic. Cook until garlic turns nut brown. Immediately add soy sauce, sugar and coriander. Add about 3/4 cup water until not too salty. (Keep sauce strong, but not overpowering.) Bring to slow boil. Mix cornstarch with cold water to make a paste. SLOWLY add cornstarch, while stirring vigorously, until sauce is thick. Poach chicken wings in water until thoroughly cooked. Toss wings in a bowl with sauce. Place on an oven pan and bake in hot oven (425 degrees) until hot and sauce is reduced to a thick glaze. This can be prepared in advance and kept cold until time of service, then placed in oven to heat. Baste wings to get more glaze.

Red Beans and Rice
Serves 4

1 onion, chopped
1 green pepper, diced
2 stalks celery, chopped
1 garlic, minced
1 tablespoon olive oil
1 tablespoon water
12 oz. can red Kidney beans, undrained
12 oz. can diced tomatoes
1 cup cooked rice
1/4 cup red wine
1/2 teaspoon crushed rosemary
1/2 teaspoon thyme
salt and pepper, to taste
tabasco, to taste

Sauté onion, pepper, celery and garlic in oil and water. Add remaining ingredients and simmer for 20 minutes. Great as a side dish or vegetarian entree.

MILETI'S

Cappellini Tuttomare
Serves 2

1/2 cup marinara sauce
2 tablespoons butter
1 tablespoon garlic, minced
1 tablespoon cilantro, chopped
1/4 cup dry white wine
6 medium large shrimp, peeled, deveined with tails on
1/2 cup squid, cleaned and cut into rings
10 fresh mussels, cleaned
10 fresh clams, cleaned
cooked angel hair pasta

Combine all ingredients, except pasta, in a medium saucepan. Cover and cook over medium-low heat until shellfish open, about 10 minutes. Serve immediately over angel hair pasta. Great with a Caesar salad, garlic bread and some nice red or white wine.

Goldener Hirsch Inn
D E E R   V A L L E Y

Saffron Risotto with Spring Vegetables
Serves 4-6

1 oz. olive oil
1 oz. butter
1 lb. arborio rice
3 pints chicken stock
1 cup white wine
1 gram saffron
2 oz. onion, diced
salt to taste
white pepper to taste
1 oz. butter
3 oz. asiago cheese

Heat oil in a saucepan. Sweat onions in oil and butter. Add rice to onions and sauté for 2 to 3 minutes over medium heat. Add stock gradually to rice. Let simmer until stock is completely absorbed before adding more stock. Add saffron to rice. Cook rice until all the stock and wine is added and rice is tender. Add salt and pepper to taste. Mix in butter and cheese. Add spring vegetable garnish.

Mulberry Street

Shrimp Pignola
Serves 1

1/2 oz. olive oil
5 jumbo shrimp
1/3 cup sliced mushrooms
1 tablespoon pine nuts
1 teaspoon chopped garlic
1/3 cup chopped tomatoes
1/2 cup clam broth
1/4 cup white wine
3 tablespoons chopped fresh basil

8 oz. linguine, cooked
freshly grated Parmesan cheese (garnish)

Sauté shrimp in olive oil until slightly pink. Add remaining ingredients except pasta and Parmesan. Heat through then serve over hot linguine. Garnish with freshly grated Parmesan cheese.

Grilled Ribeye with Black Bean Salsa
Serves 4

4 12-14 oz. ribeye steaks

Marinade:
1 cup salad oil
1 cup soy
1 cup water
1/8 cup sesame oil
1/2 bunch chopped cilantro
5 garlic cloves, crushed and minced
1/2 teaspoon black pepper

Black Bean Salsa:
3/4 cup dried black beans, washed
1/2 teaspoon salt
1 roasted red pepper, seeded, peeled
and diced
1 roasted yellow pepper, seeded, peeled
and diced
2 Chipotle chiles (canned in Adobo
Sauce), minced
1 teaspoon finely minced orange zest
1/2 teaspoon minced marjoram
1 teaspoon minced fresh cilantro
2 tablespoons sherry vinegar
2 cups extra virgin olive oil

Marinate ribeye steaks in marinade for approximately 6 hours in the refrigerator. Black Bean Salsa: Cook beans for 1 1/2 hours (or until tender). Drain and allow beans to cool. In a mixing bowl, add rest of ingredients and combine. Cook steak on hot barbecue, to a medium rare, and serve with salsa. Serving ideas: Serve with grilled fresh corn rings, grilled zucchini and oven roasted red garlic potatoes. Perfect with a good bottle of Cotes du Rhone.

Raclette Swiss Style
Serves 2

8 oz. imported Raclette cheese
6 French cornichons or small dill pickles
6 pearl onions
2 tomato wedges
2 small new potatoes, boiled

Cut the Raclette cheese into thin slices. Divide evenly on two oven-proof dishes. Place the plates under a broiler until the cheese melts, approximately 4 minutes. Garnish with boiled potatoes, cornichons, onions, tomato wedges and a dash of paprika. Serve immediately.

Veal Adolph's
Serves 2

12 oz. diced veal slices
(cut from the loin)
salt and white pepper
1 tablespoon of butter/oil
1 tablespoons diced shallots
4-6 mushrooms, sliced
1/2 cup dry white wine
1/2 cup heavy cream
1 cup veal stock
chopped parsley (garnish)

Sprinkle the diced veal with salt and pepper. Melt the butter with the oil in a skillet over medium heat. Add the shallots and diced mushrooms. Sauté for 2-3 minutes. Add the diced veal and brown lightly. Add white wine and cook for 1-2 minutes. Add cream and veal stock. Simmer all the ingredients until veal is tender (about 6-8 minutes). Season to taste. Transfer veal with sauce to a plate. Sprinkle with chopped parsley.

Swiss Rosti Potatoes
Serves 2

4-5 new potatoes
3-4 tablespoons butter
2 slices bacon, cut into small pieces
1/2 small onion, finely chopped
salt and pepper
chopped parsley (garnish)

Boil the potatoes until just tender, cool, peel and shred into large strips. In a skillet, melt the butter over medium heat. Add one half of the bacon and one half of the chopped onion. Sauté for 1-2 minutes. Add the shredded potatoes. Sprinkle liberally with salt and pepper. Top with remaining bacon and onion. Cook until the bottom of the potato patty is golden brown, 5 to 6 minutes on each side. Transfer the golden brown potatoes to a round serving platter. Sprinkle with the parsley or divide evenly on to the dinner plates. (Be sure to use a non-stick skillet for preparing this dish.)

Cherries Jubilee with Vanilla Ice Cream
Serves 2

12 dark-sweet pitted bing cherries
2 tablespoons of butter
1 tablespoon brown sugar
1 tablespoon honey
juice of 1/2 lemon
juice of 1/2 orange
1/2 oz. triple sec liquor
1/2 oz. 151-proof rum or brandy
cinnamon powder
4 large spoons of vanilla ice cream

Melt the butter in a flambé skillet over medium heat. Add the sugar, honey, lemon juice and orange juice. Cook until the ingredients are well blended and form a light syrup. Add the Triple Sec and cherries. Sauté until the cherries are warmed through. Add the rum or brandy and ignite. Sprinkle with cinnamon. Cook until the liquid is reduced to desired consistency. Spoon cherries, with liquid, over the ice cream. (If Kirsch liqueur is available, add a touch before serving.)

Herb Crusted Halibut with Tomato & Corn Salsa
Serves 4

Herb Mix:
(use all fresh herbs)
2 tablespoons chopped parsley
1 tablespoon chopped cilantro
2 tablespoons chopped basil
1 teaspoon chopped rosemary
1 teaspoon chopped oregano

4   6 oz. pieces of halibut filets

Salsa:
4 Roma tomatoes, peeled, seeded and
diced
1 ear of corn, cooked and cut from cob
1 Anaheim chili, roasted, peeled,
seeded and diced
1 shallot, diced very fine
2 tablespoons pure virgin olive oil
(not extra-virgin)
1 tablespoon lemon juice
1 teaspoon grated cumin
1 teaspoon chili powder
salt and pepper

Combine all ingredients for salsa and allow to stand in refrigerator overnight. Remove from refrigerator one hour prior to serving. Taste to adjust seasoning. Brush fish moderately with olive oil. Coat one side with herb mixture. Grill or roast in a hot skillet. Serve with salsa spooned on top of fish.

RESTAURANTS

Granola
Serves 12

4 cups quick cooking oats
1/2 cup flour
1/2 cup coconut
1/2 cup wheat germ
1 teaspoon cinnamon
1 teaspoon vanilla
1/2 cup slivered almonds
1/4 cup brown sugar
1/4 cup honey
1/2 cup vegetable oil

Thoroughly mix all ingredients in a large bowl. Make sure there are no lumps in the mixture. Spread contents onto a large cookie sheet. Bake, at 225 degrees, for 2 hours. Stir ingredients a few times while baking. Stir in raisins after the granola cools. Serve with bananas and milk at breakfast or plain for a snack.

Broccoli Salad
Serves 8

1 1/2 lb. broccoli
1 cup raisins
1 cup finely chopped red onion
1 cup sunflower seeds
7 strips bacon, crisply broiled
and crumbled

Dressing:
1 cup mayonnaise
1/3 cup sugar
2 tablespoons white vinegar

In a large bowl, combine first 5 ingredients and refrigerate. In a small bowl, combine dressing ingredients and refrigerate. Just before serving, stir dressing into salad mixture. Tasty with barbecued chicken and corn on the cob.

Lemon Bars
Serves 20

Crust:
1 1/2 cups butter
3/4 cup powdered sugar
1 1/2 teaspoon vanilla
3 cups all purpose flour

Cream together first three ingredients until smooth. Slowly add flour and mix until dough pulls together and isn't crumbly. Press into a half sheet pan and bake at 325 degrees for 20 minutes.

Filling:
6 whole eggs
3 cups granulated sugar
zest of 2 lemons
9 tablespoons lemon juice

Mix together all ingredients for filling. Pour into crust. Bake at 325 degrees for 25 minutes or until set and golden. Take out of oven. Cool. Sprinkle with powdered sugar and cut into squares.

Chicken Chile Verde
Serves 6-8

1 1/2 lb. diced chicken, raw
1/4 white onion
2 stalks celery
1 can diced green chilies
1 tablespoon diced garlic
1 teaspoon cumin
2 tablespoons canned jalapenos
cilantro (optional)
cholula hot sauce to taste
8 cups chicken stock
roux to thicken

In large stock pot, start sautéing chicken in a little oil. While chicken is cooking, place onion, celery, chilies, garlic, jalapeños and cilantro in food processor. Pulse until coarsely chopped and add to chicken and cook until tender. Add cumin and chicken stock. Bring to a rolling boil. Remove from heat. Stir in roux to thicken. Add cholula to taste. Serve over steamed rice or pour over bean and cheese burrito topped with melted cheese.

Taste of Saigon
Park City's Authentic Vietnamese Cuisine

Spicy Curry Chicken
Serves 2

1/2 lb. boneless, skinless chicken breast
2 potatoes, peeled
2 tablespoons corn oil
2 teaspoons yellow curry paste or
3 teaspoons curry powder
1 cup coconut milk
1 teaspoon brown sugar
1 teaspoon salt
1 or 2 yellow onions, quartered
1/8 teaspoon red pepper

Thinly slice chicken. Cut potatoes into 1-inch cubes. In a saucepan, heat oil and yellow curry paste on high heat. Add yellow onions, potatoes, chicken, salt and brown sugar. Stir well and cook until chicken is done and potatoes are tender. Add the coconut milk and simmer for a few more minutes. Serve immediately.

Ichiban Sushi

Gyoza
Yield: 24

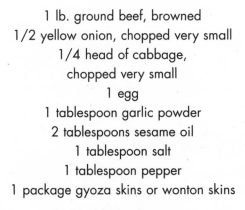

1 lb. ground beef, browned
1/2 yellow onion, chopped very small
1/4 head of cabbage,
chopped very small
1 egg
1 tablespoon garlic powder
2 tablespoons sesame oil
1 tablespoon salt
1 tablespoon pepper
1 package gyoza skins or wonton skins

Dipping Sauce

1/4 cup soy sauce, 1/4 cup rice vinegar
and layu (chili sesame oil) to taste, about
4-5 drops.

Mix all ingredients, except gyoza skins, together in a large mixing bowl. Place one teaspoon of meat mixture inside of one gyoza skin. Moisten one half of edge of skin and then fold skin in half. Press edges together to seal meat inside, then crease edges like a miniature pie shell. Repeat until meat is finished. To cook, cover bottom of a frying pan in vegetable oil and heat to medium hot. Place gyoza in pan and cook until lightly brown on one side. Turn and cook other side. Then pour 1/2 cup of water in pan and cover to steam for 1 minute. Gyoza can be frozen to cook at a later date, but be sure to dip each gyoza in cornstarch before stacking so that they don't stick together.

Miso Soup
Serves 4

5 cups water
1 teaspoon fish stock
2 tablespoons misin
(Japanese cooking wine)
2/3 cup red miso paste
1 box tofu
chopped green onions

Bring water, fish stock and cooking wine to a boil. Whisk in miso paste. Place cubes of tofu and chopped green onions in serving bowls. Ladle soup into bowls and serve while hot. Excellent source of protein.

Cilantro Shrimp
Serves 6

1/4 cup unsalted butter
3 tablespoons all purpose flour
1/4 cup finely diced onions
1/4 cup finely diced celery
2 tablespoons minced garlic
3/4 cup fish stock or clam juice
2 tablespoons minced cilantro
salt and pepper to taste
1 1/2 lb. (16-20) shrimp, peeled
and deveined
1 teaspoon fresh lime juice

Melt butter in saucepan over medium hear. When melted, stir in flour and cook, stirring constantly for 3 to 5 minutes until flour is golden brown. Add onions, celery and garlic. Continue to stir 3 to 5 minutes more. Whisk in stock or clam juice. When well blended, add cilantro and seasonings. Cook for 3 minutes. Stir in shrimp. Cover and cook for 5 minutes or until sauce is thick and flavors are blended. Add lime juice just before serving. Serve over rice or pasta.

Shrimp Scampi Style
Serves 3-4

15 black tiger shrimp, peeled and
deveined
1 tablespoon minced garlic
1 tablespoon extra virgin olive oil
2/3 cup Chablis or other wine

1 tablespoon chopped fresh herbs
(even mix of basil, chives,
oregano and parsley)
salt and pepper to taste (preferably
kosher salt and cafe grind pepper)
1 tablespoon unsalted butter
1 tablespoon fresh lemon juice
lemon (garnish)

In a skillet, heat garlic and oil over low heat for 1 minutes. Add shrimp and turn up heat. When shrimp are half done (one side bright orange), about 1 minute, turn shrimp and add the white wine and herbs. Salt and pepper to taste. When wine is completely cooked away, the shrimp will be done. At this point, add the butter and swirl rapidly in the pan until just melted. Do not over heat or sauce will separate. Serve immediately over fresh pasta. Garnish with lemon.

Beef Fajitas
Serves 8

4 lb. Flank steak, cut into 1/4" strips
(chicken or shrimp)

Marinade:
1 cup teriyaki sauce
4 Chipotle chiles
2 cups water
1 teaspoon granulated garlic
1 teaspoon black pepper
2 teaspoons red wine vinegar

2 tablespoons vegetable oil
6 green bell peppers, sliced thin
6 yellow onions, sliced thin
4 tablespoons fajita sauce
1/4 cup white wine

Fajita Spice:
1 tablespoon pasilla chili powder
1 tablespoon California chili powder
1/3 tablespoon dark chili powder
3/4 tablespoon paprika
1/3 tablespoon garlic salt
pinch each of thyme, oregano,
cumin and sugar
salt and pepper to taste

Combine marinade ingredients in a blender and puree until smooth. Marinate meat 2-12 hours or overnight. Use large skillet or wok and add vegetable oil. When hot, add meat and fajita spice. Cook meat until only a little pink is left. Add bell peppers and onions. Cook until tender. Add white wine, this will release flavors that are stuck to the bottom of skillet or pan. Cook for 1 minute. Serve fajitas right out of skillet. Serve with garnishes.

Garnishes:
shredded lettuce, shredded cheese, sour cream, guacamole, pico de gallo, lime wedges, flour tortillas

Pico de Gallo Salsa:
1 cup diced onion
1 cup diced tomato
1/2 cup diced jalapeno
1/2 cup chopped cilantro
1 teaspoon granulated garlic
pinch of salt
juice of 2 limes

Rum Cake
Serves 12

1/2 - 1 cup walnuts, crushed
1 box Duncan Hines Yellow Cake mix
1 small box vanilla instant pudding mix
1/4 cup flour
4 large eggs
1/2 cup Wesson oil
1/2 cup Dark rum
1 1/4 cup water

Sauce:
1/4 lb. butter
1 cup sugar
1/2 cup rum

Preheat oven to 350 degrees. Grease and flour a bundt pan. Add walnuts to the bottom of the pan. In large bowl beat remaining ingredients at high speed for 4 minutes. Pour cake mix into prepared pan and cook at 350 degrees, for 55-60 minutes. As soon as cake is removed from oven, in a saucepan, mix together sauce ingredients. Bring this mixture to a boil briefly. While cake is still hot, and still in the pan, poke the cake with a toothpick all over. Slowly pour the hot mixture over cake. Do not unmold cake until completely cool. Then wrap tightly with foil or plastic wrap. Best served after 2 or 3 days and will stay fresh at least 2 weeks.

ZOOM
ROADHOUSE GRILL

Pan fried Catfish with Black-eyed Peas and Collard Greens
Serves 4

Fish:
4 catfish fillets
1 cup buttermilk
2 oz. whole mustard seed
1 oz. whole fennel seed
8 oz. cornmeal
salt and pepper, to taste

Black-eyed peas:
4 oz. each red, yellow and
green bell peppers
4 oz. red onion
1 lb. black-eyed peas, soaked overnight
and cooked al dente
1 oz. garlic (puree)
1 oz. gumbo file (ground sassafras)
salt and pepper, to taste
2 quarts vegetable broth

Collard Greens:
1 lb. washed collard greens
1 oz. each garlic and shallots puree
2 quarts vegetable stock

Clean excess fat and bones from catfish. Submerge fish in buttermilk. Set aside. Grind together mustard and fennel. Add cornmeal, salt and pepper to taste. Bread the fish with cornmeal mixture. In hot oiled pan, sauté the fish until first side is golden brown. Turn and put in 350 degree oven for 5 minutes.

Sauté in hot pan peppers, onions and garlic. Add cooked black-eyed peas and lightly sauté until hot. Cover all ingredients with vegetable broth. Add gumbo file, 1/2 teaspoon vinegar, salt and pepper. Turn down heat and simmer until beans are cooked to desired texture.

In hot oiled pan, sauté garlic and shallots briefly. Add collard greens and then vegetable stock. Toss lightly until done to desired texture.

Put fish on sautéed collards with beans on the side.

Deer Valley's Apple Cobbler
Serves 20-24

5 lbs. golden delicious apples, peeled, cored and thinly sliced (about 10 apples)
1/2 cup berries, fresh or frozen
2-1/2 cups sugar, divided
2-1/4 cup flour, divided
1 cup unsalted butter, cut into bits

Butter a 9" x 13" baking pan. Combine the apples, berries, 1 cup of the sugar and 1/4 cup of the flour. Spread fruit mixture into the prepared pan. With a pastry blender, combine the remaining 1-1/2 cups sugar, 2 cups of flour and the butter until the mixture forms a fine meal. Sprinkle over the fruit mixture. Bake, at 350 degrees, for 1 hour or until the topping is golden brown and the fruit is bubbling.

AT DEER VALLEY

Sun-Dried Tomato and Pesto Mascarpone Terrine
Serves 16

Mascarpone Cheese:
1 1/2 lbs. cream cheese, softened
1 lb. whole butter, softened
2 teaspoons black pepper
1/2 teaspoon salt

Pesto:
2 cups fresh basil leaves, tightly packed
1/2 cup pine nuts, toasted
1/2 cup Parmesan cheese, grated
1/4 cup garlic, minced
1/2 cup olive oil
1 teaspoon salt
2 teaspoons black pepper

Dried Tomato Puree:
2 cups sun-dried tomatoes
1 tablespoon marjoram, chopped
2 teaspoons garlic, minced
1 teaspoon black pepper

Combine cheese ingredients and puree in food processor until smooth. Set aside. Combine pesto ingredients and blend in food processor until smooth but still particulate. Set aside. For dried tomato puree, blend ingredients in food processor until smooth.

For terrine: Line a 4-6 cup deep serving bowl (or mixing bowl) with plastic wrap so about 2" hangs over the rim. Make the wrap as wrinkle free as possible on the inside of the bowl. Begin filling the bowl with alternating layers of ingredients until last ingredient (cheese) is 1/4" from the top of the bowl. Spoon in the first bottom layer: 1/2" cheese, then 1/4" pesto, then 1/2" cheese, then 1/4" tomato puree, then repeat. Smooth out each layer with spoon to make layers level. After adding a layer, tap base of bowl firmly on table to eliminate air pockets. When final layer is added, cover with plastic wrap and refrigerate 4 hours.

To serve, remove cover of plastic wrap and invert onto serving platter. If the terrine does not unmold by itself, pull the edges of the plastic wrap liner to help remove it from the bowl. Once unmolded, remove plastic wrap and arrange your favorite crackers or toasts around the terrine.

Swedish Meatballs

Serves 4-6

1 tablespoon plus 1 teaspoon margarine, divided
3/4 cup minced onion
1 cup cream, divided
1 egg
1/2 cup oatmeal
15 oz. ground beef
4 oz. ground pork
2 teaspoons salt, divided
1 1/2 teaspoons sugar, divided
1/2 teaspoon allspice
1/2 teaspoon ground nutmeg
3 tablespoons all purpose flour
1/4 teaspoon white pepper
2 cups milk
(or 1 cup milk and 1 cup water)
1/4 teaspoon paprika

Preheat oven to 350 degrees. In small skillet heat 1 teaspoon margarine; add onion and sauté until golden. Transfer to mixing bowl and add 1/4 cup cream, the egg and oatmeal, stirring well to combine. Let stand for 5 minutes. Add meat and 1 teaspoon each of sugar and salt, allspice and nutmeg. Using a fork, blend well. Using a teaspoon, form meat mixture into small balls about 1/2 inch in diameter. Set on rack in roasting pan and bake, turning once, for 10 minutes. Remove from oven and set aside. In 2-quart saucepan heat remaining table-spoon margarine until bubbly and hot. Add flour and cook over low heat stirring constantly for 3 minutes. Stir in remaining 3/4 cup cream. Add milk, remaining tea-spoon salt and 1/2 teaspoon sugar, paprika, and pepper. Cook stirring constantly until thick. Add meatballs and cook until heated.

Lemon Waffles
(Vafler med sitronsmak)
Yield: 6 waffles

5 eggs
1/2 cup sugar
1 cup flour
1 tsp. lemon juice, fresh
1/2 teaspoon lemon peel, freshly grated
1 cup sour cream
1/2 cup butter

Beat eggs and sugar until thick and fluffy, about ten minutes. Alternately fold in the flour, sifted with lemon peel and the sour cream. Stir in the butter and lemon juice. Set batter aside to rest 10-15 minute. Heat heart-shaped waffle iron. Pour approximately 3/4-cup batter in the center of the iron. Lower cover and bake until the steaming stops (30-60 seconds).

Red Onion & Curry Dressing
Yield: 2 cups

1/2 cup mayonnaise
1/2 cup sour cream
3/4 cup small curd cottage cheese
1/4 cup milk
1/2 teaspoon curry powder
salt and pepper to taste
1/4 small red onion, diced (if onion has strong aroma, lessen the amount)

In a blender, combine the mayonnaise, sour cream, cottage cheese and milk until smooth. Add the spices and red onion and blend until the texture of the red onion meets personal preference. Taste. If a stronger onion flavor is desired, add more red onion.

WASHINGTON SCHOOL INN

Eggs Florentine
Serves 8

12 eggs
2 cups cottage cheese
1 cup grated Swiss cheese
(packed tightly)
4 oz. Feta cheese, cubed small
4 oz. cream cheese
10 oz. frozen chopped spinach,
thawed and drained
1/2 teaspoon nutmeg
1/4 cup toasted almond slivers (optional)
1/4 cup Parmesan cheese (optional)

Beat eggs lightly. Stir in spinach and nutmeg. Add cheeses and mix. Pour into 2 greased pie plates. Top with almonds (optional). Bake at 375 degrees (bottom shelf) for 1 hour or until knife comes out clean in center. Cool 5-10 minutes before cutting.

Grilled Ahi Tuna
with Citrus Sauce
Serves 8

RIVERHORSE
cafe

8 tuna steaks
1/4 cup fresh squeezed lemon juice
1/4 cup fresh squeezed lime juice
1 cup fresh squeezed grapefruit juice
1 cup fresh squeezed orange juice
2 shallots, peeled and minced
1 lb. unsalted butter
olive oil
white pepper
cayenne pepper
fresh ground black pepper
chopped chives for garnish

Sweat the shallots in a saucepan with a little butter. When they become translucent (but not browned), add the juices. Reduce the liquid until it is of a syrupy consistency (about as thick as you would like the sauce to be). With the sauce barely simmering whisk in bits of whole butter little by little until it is all incorporated. Season with salt, white pepper and cayenne. Strain and keep warm (if sauce becomes too hot or too cool the butter will separate and the sauce with "break"). Coat tuna steaks with olive oil. Season with salt and black pepper and grill to medium rare. Serve tuna steaks with the citrus sauce, sprinkled with chopped chives.

**STEIN ERIKSEN
LODGE**

Potato Lasagna
Serves 4

2 Idaho russet potatoes, peeled
8 oz. sliced shitake mushrooms
8 oz. oyster mushrooms
4 oz. butter mushrooms, sliced
1 tablespoon chives
2 egg whites
1 lb. leeks, diced
1 lb. celery, diced
1 lb. onions, diced
14 oz. white wine
diced tomato (garnish)
chives (garnish)

Cook potatoes whole for 15 minutes. Cool and grate. Sauté mushrooms in butter with salt and pepper. Set aside. Add chives to grated potato plus 2 egg whites to form a pancake. Sauté in hot skillet until crisp, set aside with the sautéed mushrooms in between two pancakes. Put leeks, celery and onions in stock pot with wine. Reduce by one half and add 8 oz. of water. Reduce by one half again. Set aside to cool, then strain. Bring liquid back to boil, then simmer. Whisk in 2 oz. butter until emulsified. Set pancakes with mushrooms in center of plate and drizzle sauce around. Garnish with diced tomatoes and diced chives.

Beer Battered Jalapeño Poppers
Yield: 30 poppers

fresh jalapeno
8 oz. cream cheese
1 bunch fresh cilantro
2 oz. black olives
1/2 tablespoon Tabasco
32 oz. fry oil

Beer Batter:
1 can cold beer
1 cup all purpose flour
1/2 cup cornstarch
1 tablespoon paprika
pinch of garlic salt
salt and pepper to taste

In food processor, combine cream cheese, black olives, fresh cilantro and Tabasco. Blend until smooth. Set aside. With a paring knife make slit in the length of the pepper. Pinch the pepper between two fingers using the top and bottom so the pepper opens slightly. Using a spoon remove seeds. Stuff pepper with cream cheese mixture. Mix ingredients of beer batter. Preheat fry oil to 325 degrees. Dip stuffed jalapeno pepper into beer batter, then place into fry oil (Be careful of the oil splatter). Serve golden brown with salsa, sour cream or guacamole.

The Eating Establishment's Famous Beer Bread
Yield: 4 loaves

12 cups Gold Medal self-rising flour
1 cup granulated sugar
72 oz. beer
1/2 cup melted butter

Combine dry ingredients. Add beer to consistency of thick batter. Spray 4 bread pans (10" x 5" x 3") with no stick pan coating. Fill bread pans 3/4 full. Bake in preheated oven at 350 degrees for approximately 45 minutes. Test if done with a tooth pick. Remove from pans, brush lightly with butter. Let cool and wrap.

WASATCH BREW PUB

Lamb Marengo
Serves 12-16

5 lb. diced lamb
1/4 cup olive oil
1/4 cup chopped garlic
1 quart onions
1 tablespoon whole dried thyme
1 tablespoon white pepper
3 1/2 oz. chopped fresh rosemary
1 cup tomato paste
2 quarts mushrooms, quartered
3 cups red wine
3 cups chicken stock
5 lb. canned tomatoes, diced
1/4 cup balsamic vinegar

Brown lamb in convection oven. To olive oil, add lamb, garlic, onions, thyme, white pepper and rosemary. Cook until onions are soft. Add tomato paste and mushrooms. Cook for 8-10 minutes. Add red wine and cook for 5 minutes. Add chicken stock and diced tomatoes. Simmer for 15-20 minutes. Finish with balsamic vinegar and remove from heat.

THE YARROW

Vegetable Lasagna
Serves 4

1 eggplant
2 yellow squash
2 zucchini
1 yellow pepper
1 green pepper
1 red pepper
1 red onion
6 roma tomatoes, diced
4 cloves garlic, minced
1/2 teaspoon thyme
1/2 teaspoon powdered rosemary
2 tablespoons olive oil
1/4 cup balsamic vinegar

4 spinach pasta sheets, 6-inches wide
2 cups marinara sauce
fresh basil leaves (garnish)
Parmesan cheese (garnish)

Slice eggplant, squashes, peppers and red onion in 1/2-inch slices and grill until partially cooked. Let cool and dice. Mix with tomatoes, garlic and herbs. Sauté vegetable mixture in olive oil for 5 minutes and add balsamic vinegar. Poach pasta sheets. Place each sheet in the middle of the plate and put a large spoonful of mixture toward one end. Fold pasta over and repeat process until you have three layers with pasta on top. Ladle 1/2 cup warm marinara sauce on to center of each pasta. Garnish with basil leaves and shredded Parmesan.

APPETIZERS

Inside General Store

*Appetizers, the main course and almost everything
else could be purchased in Park City's general
stores. These stores were a combination of grocery,
dry goods and sometimes even meat markets. A few
of the more popular stores were called Welsh,
Driscoll and Buck's, Paul Bros., Wilson's, and
Blyth-Fargo The Big Store. During the late 1880's,
it cost $4-$5 for one hundred pounds of flour,
unsliced bacon was forty cents a pound and Irish
potatoes were sold for "four bits a bushel."*

Holiday Shrimp Dip
Serves 8

8 oz. cream cheese
1 cup mayonnaise
1 teaspoon unsalted garlic powder
1 teaspoon sea salt
1 tablespoon cocktail sauce
4 oz. can whole, tiny shrimp

Put ingredients, except shrimp, into the bowl of a food processor. Process until light, fluffy and well blended. Transfer mixture to mixing bowl. Carefully fold in drained shrimp until well distributed throughout. Serve with chips for dipping.

Italian Salsa
Yield: 2 cups

1/2 cup (dry pack) sundried tomatoes
1 medium shallot, minced
2 cloves garlic, minced
3 Roma tomatoes, seeded and chopped
1/2 cup basil leaves
2 tablespoons olive oil
1/2 teaspoon salt
1/4 teaspoon white pepper
Goat cheese
Water biscuits

Mix first eight ingredients together. Do not use a food processor. Serve with goat cheese and water biscuits.

Ron's Crab Rounds
Yield: 3-4 dozen

8 oz. canned crab, drained
1 cup grated Parmesan cheese
3 teaspoons chopped green onion
1/2 teaspoon garlic powder
1/2 teaspoon curry powder
mayonnaise, to moisten
1 package butterflake rolls

Mix first 6 ingredients together. Take apart butterflake rolls (so you have a wafer like slice). Place roll slice on cookie sheet. Top with crab mixture. Bake, at 350 degrees, for 15 minutes.

Avocado Paté
Yield: 4 cups

1 cup chutney
2" sliced ginger, peeled
1/2 jalapeno pepper, seeded
1/3 cup pistachio nuts
1/4 cup parsley
1/4 cup cilantro

3 ripe avocados, pureed
16 oz. cream cheese
1 1/4 tablespoon lime juice
1/4 teaspoon cayenne pepper
1/2 teaspoon salt
Chips

Line loaf pan with avocado oil. Mix first 6 ingredients in food processor and set aside. Mix next 5 ingredients together. Pour one half avocado puree into prepared pan. Add 1/3 chutney mixture, then one half avocado puree and 1/3 chutney mixture. Refrigerate overnight. Unmold, covering with remaining 1/3 chutney mixture. Serve with chips.

Chili con Queso
Serves 8

2 large onions, diced
2 tablespoons butter
1 28 oz. can whole tomatoes, diced
2 4 oz. cans diced green chilies
1 cup heavy cream
1 lb. Monterey Jack cheese
salt, to taste
tortilla chips

Cook onions in butter over low heat. Add tomatoes and chilies and cook until thick. Cool and stir in cream, cheese and salt. Cook gently until cheese melts. Serve with tortilla chips.

Bacon Wrapped Dates
Serves 8

16 whole pitted dates
16 pecan halves
8 slices bacon cut in half

Take a pitted date, stuff a pecan half inside and wrap with 1/2 strip of lean bacon. Place on jelly roll pan. Bake, at 375 degrees, until bacon is done (approximately 15-20 minutes). Drain on paper towels.

Roasted Garlic & Almond Dip
Yield: 2 1/2 cups

3 heads garlic, peeled
(about 36-40 cloves)
1/4 cup vegetable oil
2 teaspoons Worcestershire sauce
1 1/2 cups blanched almonds, toasted
and coarsely chopped (about 6 oz.)
1 cup sour cream
1 cup mayonnaise
1/4 cup plus 2 tablespoons chopped
fresh parsley
2 teaspoons dried rosemary, crumbled
salt and pepper to taste
crackers
fresh vegetables

Position rack in lowest third of oven and preheat oven to 300 degrees. Place garlic in small baking dish and toss with oil. Bake until garlic is soft and golden, about 30 minutes. Transfer to blender and let cool, about 30 minutes. Add Worcestershire sauce and mustard to garlic and blend until garlic is finely chopped. Scrape mixture into large bowl. Stir in almonds, sour cream, mayonnaise and herbs. Season with salt and pepper. Cover and refrigerate at least 2 hours or overnight to mellow flavors. Let stand at room temperature for 1 hour before serving. Serve with crackers and fresh vegetables.

Tomato Horseradish Dipping Sauce
Yield: 1 1/2 cups

1 cup ketchup
2 tablespoons lemon juice
1/4 cup drained bottled horseradish
2 tablespoons Worcestershire sauce
1/4 teaspoon hot red pepper flakes
1/4 cup fresh cilantro, minced
1/2 cup celery, minced
2 scallions, minced
cilantro for garnish

Stir together the ketchup, lemon juice, horseradish, Worcestershire sauce, red pepper flakes, cilantro, celery and the scallions until the mixture is combined well. Transfer the sauce to a serving bowl and chill it, covered, for at least 1 hour or up to 24 hours. Garnish with cilantro. Serve with shrimp, crab claws and/or vegetables.

Clam Dip in a Bread
Serves 30

4   6 oz. cans chopped clams
1 cup clam juice
4   8 oz. packages cream cheese
15 drops of tabasco sauce
2 tablespoons lemon juice
1 teaspoon garlic powder
1 large round bread

Drain clams and keep 1 cup of the clam juice. Mix all ingredients together. Cut a circle around top of bread and remove inside of bread carefully. Put the mixed ingredients inside the bread. Wrap securely in foil. Cook for 3 hours at 325 degrees. Serve hot with vegetables and/or bread pieces.

Cocktail Meatballs
Yield: 60 meatballs

2 lb. lean turkey burger
(or lean ground beef)
1 cup bread crumbs
1/3 cup parsley flakes
2 eggs
2 tablespoons soy sauce
3 tablespoon onion flakes
1/4 teaspoon pepper
pinch of garlic powder

Sauce:
16 oz. can jellied cranberry sauce
1   12 oz. jar chili sauce
2 tablespoons lemon juice
2 tablespoons brown sugar

Mix turkey, bread crumbs, parsley flakes, eggs, soy sauce, onion flakes, pepper and garlic powder. Form mixture into small balls. Place in 9" x 13" pan with 6 meatballs across and 10 meatballs down. Bake, uncovered, for 30 minutes at 350 degrees. Heat sauce ingredients until smooth. Serve warm with meatballs.

Easy Homemade Salsa
Yield: 4 cups

fresh cilantro
2 small cans "El Pato" Mexican style
tomato sauce
15 oz. can of Mexican stewed tomatoes
1 medium onion, peeled
and cut into chunks
4 - 5 cloves garlic, minced
salt and pepper to taste
splash of lime juice
tortilla chips

In a blender, combine the first 7 ingredients. Chill and serve with tortilla chips.

Salsa
Yield: 2-3 cups

4 - 6 tomatoes, peeled, seeded and
chopped
chopped green onions
1/4 - 1/2 bunch of cilantro
1-2 cloves garlic, minced
1 Anaheim chili pepper,
seeded and chopped
1 tablespoon olive oil
1 tablespoon lemon juice
salt and pepper

Mix and serve with chicken as a marinade or on French bread.

Tomato Bruschetta with Basil
Serves 6

2 cups diced tomatoes
1/4 cup fresh basil, lightly packed
2 clove garlic, minced
1/2 loaf French bread or Italian bread
1 tablespoon olive oil
2 tablespoons Parmesan cheese, grated

Combine tomato, basil, minced garlic and salt and pepper. Let stand 15 minutes, then cover and refrigerate for 4 hours. Slice bread on an angle in 1-inch slices. Broil on each side until lightly browned. Rub halved garlic over bread and brush with olive oil. Spoon refrigerated mixture over top and sprinkle with Parmesan cheese. Broil for 1 minute and serve. Can also be served without broiling.

Mexican Dip
Yield: 10 cups

1 1/2 lb. ground beef
1 1/2 lb. pork sausage
2 lb. Velveeta cheese
8 oz. chopped green chilies
jalapenos to taste (1-2)
15 oz. tomato sauce
6 oz. tomato paste

Brown meat in skillet and drain excess fat. In large kettle, combine meat and remaining ingredients. Cook over medium heat until the cheese has melted. Serve with tortilla chips. Freezes well.

Filled Brie with Pinon Nuts
Serves 8

1 lb. pie-shaped wedge of brie
1/3 cup pesto sauce
sun dried tomatoes
1-2 tablespoons butter, melted
pinon nuts, chopped

Make pesto sauce with basil leaves, garlic and oil or use purchased pesto. Chop sun-dried tomatoes, packed in oil, slightly in food processor. Slice cheese in half to produce two pie wedges. Spread tomato mixture on one side of brie and pesto mixture on the other side. Put both pieces together. Spread top very lightly with butter and sprinkle with pinon nuts. Serve at room temperature with crackers.

Bacon Roll-Ups
Serves 4

4 oz. cream cheese
1/4 cup sour cream
2 tablespoons chives
dash garlic salt
2 tablespoons Parmesan cheese
1 loaf sliced wheat bread
1 package lean bacon

Cream together cream cheese, sour cream, chives, garlic salt and Parmesan cheese. Set aside. Cut crust from bread. Roll bread, with rolling pin, until thin. Spread with cream cheese mixture. Cut bread piece in half. Wrap outside of bread with one half a strip of bacon. Secure with toothpick. Bake, in broiler pan, at 400 degrees for 10 minutes on each side.

Sun Dried Tomato Dip
Yield: 1 cup

1 oz. sun dried tomatoes,
soaked and chopped
1/2 cup Canadian bacon, diced
1/2 cup fat free cream cheese
1/4 cup non fat or low fat sour cream
1 clove garlic, chopped
1/2 tablespoon chopped basil

Mix above ingredients and serve with crackers.

Salmon Ball
Serves 8-10

1 can red salmon
1 tablespoon horseradish
1/4 teaspoon salt
2 teaspoon grated onion
1 tablespoon lemon juice
8 oz. package cream cheese
1/4 teaspoon liquid smoke
finely chopped nuts
parsley flakes

Combine first 7 ingredients and mix well. Shape into a ball. Chill. Roll in mixture of finely chopped nuts and parsley flakes. Serve with crackers.

Chilled Mussels with Curry Mayonnaise

Yield: 24 hors d'oeuvres

1/4 cup dry white wine
24 mussels, scrubbed well
and beards scraped off
1/4 cup curry mayonnaise
1 1/2 teaspoons minced fresh chives

Curry Mayonnaise:
1 cup mayonnaise
1 tablespoon curry powder
1 teaspoon mussel cooking liquid or
bottled clam juice
1 1/4 teaspoon fresh lemon juice

In a large saucepan, boil wine 1 minute and add mussels. Steam mussels, covered, stirring once or twice, 2 to 5 minutes, or until most have opened, discarding any unopened mussels. Cool mussels in cooking liquid until they can be handled and remove from shells, reserving about 1 tablespoon liquid in a small bowl and one half shell from each mussel. Gently pull off and discard black rims of mussels, if desired. To serve, arrange half shells on plates and put curry mayonnaise into each shell. Top with a mussel and decorate with 1/4 teaspoon mayonnaise and a sprinkle of chives.

Curry Mayonnaise: In a bowl, stir ingredients together until combined well. Chill, covered, for 30 minutes. Mayonnaise will keep in refrigerator, covered, for up to one week. To decorate with mayonnaise use a pastry bag or a plastic bag with the corner snipped 1/8".

Guacamole, Not!

Yield: 1 cup

1 large can cut asparagus, drained
1.1 oz. package dry Ranch dressing mix
juice of 1 lemon
1 tablespoon minced onion
dash of Tabasco sauce
chips
raw vegetables

Combine all ingredients in the blender and whirl. Serve with raw vegetable or chips for dipping.

Basil Tomato Appetizer
Serves 8

1/2 cup sun dried tomatoes, chopped
1/2 cup fresh tomatoes, finely chopped
1 clove garlic, minced
1/2 teaspoon olive oil
1/2 cup goat cheese
1/3 cup no fat sour cream
fresh basil leaves
melba rounds

To soften sun dried tomatoes, cover with water and place in a small bowl. Heat in a microwave on high for 1 minute. If still firm, continue to microwave 30 seconds more. Drain. Chop and mix with fresh tomato, garlic and olive oil. Place in a small dish for serving. Mix together goat cheese and sour cream and put in another small dish for serving. Wash basil leaves, dry and remove stems. On a large plate, place the dishes of tomato mixture and goat cheese mixture. Surround with the fresh basil leaves. Spread a melba round with goat cheese, a dollop of tomato mixture and top with a fresh basil leaf.

Apolonia's Egg Rolls
Serves 8-10

Egg Roll Filling:
1 lb. ground pork, beef or chicken
2 carrots, chopped
2 celery stalks, chopped
1 onion, chopped
2 cups shredded cabbage
1 clove garlic, crushed
salt and pepper to taste
1 cup chopped bell pepper
1 teaspoon sugar
1 package egg roll wrappers
2 cups oil for frying
1 cup water for sealing the wrappers

Mix together the filling ingredients and set aside for 30 minutes. Place 1 tablespoon of meat filling on each wrapper. Roll as directed on the package, sealing end of wrapper with water. Heat oil on medium high temperature. Fry egg rolls in oil until brown on both sides. Serve warm with fruit dipping sauce.

Fruit Dipping Sauce:
1/2 cup catsup
1/2 cup fruit preserves, any flavor

Blend well and transfer to serving dish.

Spinach Cheese Dip with Pita Chips
Serves 8

10 oz. package frozen chopped
spinach, thawed and drained
8 oz. package cream
cheese, softened
1 teaspoon grated onion
1 medium tomato, diced
1 cup Monterey Jack cheese, grated
1 beaten egg

Mix ingredients together. Bake at 350 degrees for 20 minutes or until heated through.

Pita Chips:
1/2 cup melted butter or margarine
1 tablespoon cumin
1 tablespoon lemon pepper
1 package pita bread, cut into triangles

Melt butter with cumin and lemon pepper. Toss pita triangles in butter mixture. Bake in a single layer, at 375 degrees, until lightly browned and crisp (about 20 minutes).

Artichoke Dip
Serves 8-10

8 oz. can non-marinated artichoke
hearts, drained and chopped
1/2 cup sour cream
1/2 cup mayonnaise
8 oz. package cream
cheese, softened
1 cup grated Parmesan cheese
1 clove garlic, minced
dill weed to taste

Mix together all ingredients except artichoke hearts and beat until smooth. Add artichoke hearts. Place in a greased pie or quiche pan. Bake, at 350 degrees, for 20 minutes. Serve with crackers.

Cheese Stuffed Mushrooms
Serves 8

6 tablespoons butter or
margarine, melted
16 slices French bread, 1/2 inch thick
16 large mushrooms, stems removed
2 tablespoons freshly squeezed
lemon juice
1 large egg
2/3 lb. Stilton or Bleu cheese, crumbled
16 large walnut pieces
parsley sprigs

Preheat oven to 400 degrees. Line a large baking sheet with aluminum foil. Lightly butter both sides of bread using 4 table-spoons of the butter. Bake bread pieces for 5 minutes, turning once. Remove from oven and side aside. In large bowl, toss mushroom caps in fresh lemon juice. Drain. Discard juice. Place 2 tablespoons melted butter in bowl, add mushroom caps and toss. Place one cap, stem side up on each slice of toast-ed bread. In small bowl, beat egg with fork. Stir in cheese. Spoon cheese mixture into mushroom caps, dividing evenly. Broil mushroom caps about 8 to 10 inches from heat source for 5 to 6 minutes or until gold-en brown. Place walnut piece or parsley sprig on each mushroom before serving.

Bruschetta
Serves 8-10

6 cloves garlic, finely diced
3/4 cup olive oil
8-10 roma tomatoes
25 leaves fresh basil
1/4 cup grated Parmesan cheese
20 1/2" slices French bread

With clean fingers, combine garlic with olive oil in a bowl. Liberally rub bread with garlic oil on top side, allowing for occasional chunk garlic to remain on bread. Broil bread in oven on cookie sheet until browned. Cube tomatoes, slice basil ribbons and combine with grated cheese and garlic oil. Roll and tumble entire medley with hands until oil travels evenly. Pile medley on cooled toast (approximately 1 tablespoon per slice).

Santa Fe Dip
Yield: 3 cups

2　4 oz. cans chopped green chilies
2　4 1/2 oz. cans chopped black olives
3 tomatoes, chopped
3 green onions, chopped
2 tablespoons wine vinegar
1 tablespoon vegetable or olive oil
salt and pepper to taste

Combine green chilies with olives, tomatoes, green onions, wine vinegar, oil, salt and pepper in medium bowl, blending well. Serve immediately or refrigerate overnight to heighten flavors.

Herb and Spice Coated Cheese Balls
Yield: 6 dozen cheese balls

Coriander-Cumin Cheese Balls:
1/3 cup finely chopped coriander
(cilantro), parsley or watercress
1 teaspoon ground cumin
1 1/4 lb. Jarlsberg cheese
1 tablespoon melted butter or margarine

Ginger-Sesame Cheese Balls:
1/3 cup sesame sees, toasted
1 1/4 teaspoon ground ginger
1 1/4 teaspoon soy sauce
1 1/4 lb. mozzarella cheese
1 tablespoon melted butter or margarine

Paprika-Pistachio Cheese Balls:
4 teaspoons finely ground pistachio nuts
2 1/2 teaspoons paprika
1 1/4 lb. Cheddar cheese

Prepare Coriander-Cumin cheese balls: Mix coriander and cumin in small bowl until well blended; set aside. Using a melon baller, scoop out balls of cheese from wedge of Jarlsberg. With wooden pick, dip a cheese ball into melted butter, letting excess liquid drip off. Sprinkle coriander-cumin mixture over entire ball, patting to help coating adhere. Place on a platter. Cover and refrigerate until ready to serve.
Prepare Ginger-Sesame Cheese Balls: Mix sesame seed, ginger and soy sauce in small bowl until well blended. Make balls using same procedure as above except using mozzarella cheese and ginger-sesame coating.
Prepare Paprika-Pistachio Cheese Balls: Mix ground nuts and paprika in small bowl. Make balls using cheddar cheese. Roll in nut mixture.

Chicken Twists with Tarragon Avocado Dipping Sauce
Serves 10

1 lb. boneless chicken breasts, skinned and split, pounded to 1/4" thick
1 lb. boneless chicken thighs, skinned, pounded to 1/4" thick
1 1/2 cup unsifted all purpose flour
2 cups fine dry unseasoned bread crumbs
2 large eggs, beaten with 2 1/2 tablespoons water
vegetable oil for deep-frying

Tarragon-Avocado Dipping Sauce:
1 ripe avocado, pitted and cubed
1 cup sour cream
1/4 cup freshly squeezed lime juice
1 1/2 tablespoon honey
3 tablespoons fresh tarragon leaves or
1 tablespoon dried tarragon leaves
1 teaspoon salt
1/8 teaspoon pepper
lime slices (optional garnish)
sprig of tarragon (optional garnish)

Cut chicken pieces diagonally into strips 1" x 4". Place flour and bread crumbs in separate pie plates. Put egg mixture in a medium sized bowl. Coat each chicken strip with flour, shaking off excess, set aside. Dip floured chicken one at a time in egg mixture, then coat with bread crumbs. Twist chicken strip gently and place on tray. Refrigerate 30 minutes. Pour enough vegetable oil into a Dutch oven to measure 3 inches. Heat over moderately high heat until oil registers 365 degrees on a deep-fat thermometer. Add 5 coated chicken twists to the hot oil. Fry until cooked through and golden brown, approximately 30 seconds. Remove chicken twists and drain on paper towel. Transfer chicken to tray and refrigerate until ready to serve. Prepare dipping sauce by placing all the ingredients in a food processor and puree until smooth. Garnish dip with lime slices and a sprig of tarragon.

Peking Chicken Wings
Yield: 30

3 lb. chicken wings, tips removed
salt and pepper to taste
2 tablespoon vegetable oil
1 cup honey
3/4 cup soy sauce
2 tablespoons ketchup
1 clove garlic, mashed
parsley (optional garnish)

Preheat oven to 375 degrees. Halve chicken wings. Place in 9" x 12" shallow baking dish. Sprinkle with salt, pepper and vegetable oil. Combine honey, soy sauce, ketchup and mashed garlic in a 2-cup measure, blending well. Pour over chicken, coating evenly. Bake in oven for 50 minutes or until bubbly. Garnish with parsley.

Burns and Carpenter's Snow Park Resort
(Future home of Deer Valley)

*Nothing tastes better than a bowl of hot soup
or stew after a long, cold day of skiing. In 1946,
Bob Burns and Otto Carpenter built Park City's
first official ski resort, Snow Park, named after the
Snow Park Ski Club. The resort featured chair lifts
and ski runs for beginning and advanced skiers.
La Rue Carpenter, Otto's wife, operated a small
warming hut which featured good, hot food at
reasonable prices. Adult ski passes sold for $2.50;
children passes were $1.00. Although Snow Park
Resort closed in 1969, it lives on at Deer Valley Ski
Resort where the base lodge is named Snow Park,
one chair lift is named Burns and another is
named Carpenter.*

Curried Peanut Soup

Serves 4-6

3 tablespoons butter
1 small onion, diced
1 medium carrot, diced
1 large stalk celery, diced
1 teaspoon curry powder, or to taste
2 tablespoons whole wheat flour
4 cups vegetable or chicken stock
1/2 cup peanut butter
2 tablespoons catsup
2 teaspoons Worcestershire sauce
1 cup cooked brown rice

1/2 cup sour cream (garnish)
1/2 cup chopped peanuts (garnish)

Melt butter in a 3-quart pan over medium heat. Add onion, carrot and celery. Cook, stirring occasionally until vegetables are soft, about 10 minutes. Stir in curry powder and cook for 1 minute. Stir in flour and cook 1 minute more. Gradually stir in stock. Reduce heat, cover and simmer for 15 minutes. Stir in peanut butter, catsup and Worcestershire sauce until smooth. Add rice and simmer, uncovered, for 5 minutes. Garnish each serving with a spoonful of sour cream and chopped peanuts.

Artichoke Soup

Serves 8

1 can cream of mushroom soup
1 can cream of celery soup
2 1/2 soup cans milk
5 oz. can shrimp, drained (optional)
1 cup finely shredded carrots
14 oz. can artichoke hearts, drained
and coarsely chopped
1/2 teaspoon curry powder
dash seasoned pepper
dash ground allspice
1/4 teaspoon onion powder

Combine all ingredients in deep saucepan and simmer uncovered for 15 minutes. Serve immediately.

Crab and Corn Bisque
Serves 8

1/2 cup chopped celery
1/2 cup chopped green onions
1/4 cup chopped green pepper
1/2 cup butter or margarine, melted
2   10 3/4 oz. cans cream of potato
soup, undiluted
15 oz. can cream-style corn
1 1/2 cups half and half
1 1/2 cups milk
2 bay leaves
1 teaspoon dried whole thyme
1/2 teaspoon garlic powder
1/4 teaspoon white pepper
dash of hot sauce
1 lb. lump crab meat

chopped parsley (optional)
lemon slices (optional)

Sauté celery, green onions and green pepper in butter in a heavy Dutch oven. Add soup and next 8 ingredients, cook until thoroughly heated. Gently stir in crab meat, and heat thoroughly. Discard bay leaves. Garnish with parsley and lemon slices, if desired.

Red Pepper Soup
Serves 4

14 oz. can pimento, drained
2 1/2 cups vegetable broth
salt and freshly ground pepper, to taste
1 tablespoon ground coriander
1/2 lb. cooked pasta shapes
fresh coriander to garnish

Place pimento in a food processor or blender and puree until smooth. Transfer to a large saucepan and add the vegetable broth, salt, pepper and ground coriander. Stir and cook over gentle heat for about 10 minutes. Add the cooked pasta shapes and cook for 2 to 3 minutes. Serve warm, garnished with fresh coriander.

Curried Onion Soup
Serves 6-8

2 tablespoon butter
1 tablespoon curry powder
2 onions, sliced
8 cups chicken broth, diluted
1/2 cup rice
bay leaf

chopped parsley (optional)
sour cream (optional)

Melt butter, add curry and stir for a few minutes. Add onion, broth, rice and bay leaf. Cook for 20-25 minutes. Add rice and cook for another 20-25 minutes. Remove bay leaf. Strain and puree ingredients. Reheat and garnish with chopped parsley and a dollop of sour cream (optional).

Mexican Corn Soup
Serves 4-6

3 tablespoons butter
1/3 cup chopped green pepper
1/4 cup sliced green onion
1 large clove garlic, minced
5 tablespoons flour
1/4 teaspoon oregano
1/4 teaspoon pepper
2 to 3 drops Tabasco sauce
2 cups milk
1 cup condensed chicken broth
1 bay leaf
2 cups (8 oz.) shredded Monterey Jack cheese, divided
1 1/2 cups red salsa, mild to medium
1 1/2 cups fresh or frozen corn

Tortilla chips
cilantro (garnish)

Melt butter in 3-quart saucepan. Sauté green pepper, onion and garlic until tender (about 5 minutes). Stir in flour, oregano, pepper and Tabasco sauce. Gradually stir in milk and broth. Add bay leaf. Bring to boiling, stirring constantly. Boil and stir 1 minute. Remove from heat. Stir in 1 1/2 cups cheese, salsa and corn until cheese is melted. Remove bay leaf. Garnish each serving with tortilla chips, a little shredded cheese and cilantro. Serve immediately.

Green Chile Soup
Serves 6

3 bell peppers, seeded and cut
in 1-inch pieces
3 green chilies, roasted and peeled
1 small onion, diced
4 cups chicken stock
2 tablespoons butter
2 tablespoons flour
1 cup cream or evaporated milk
salt and pepper to taste
sour cream (garnish)

Puré peppers, chilies and onions in food processor or blender with 1 cup of the stock. Melt butter, blend in flour, gradually stir in chili mixture and chicken stock. Bring to a boil and simmer gently, stirring constantly, until soup is smooth. Blend in cream or undiluted evaporated milk. Heat through but do not boil. Add salt and pepper to taste. Serve topped with sour cream and slice of green pepper.

Italian Sausage Soup
Serves 10

1 1/2 lb. hot Italian sausage, crumbled
2 cloves garlic, minced
2 onions, chopped
2 (1 lb.) cans Italian plum tomatoes
and juice
1 1/2 cup dry red wine
5 cups beef broth
1/2 teaspoon dried basil
1/2 teaspoon dried oregano
3 tablespoons fresh parsley, chopped
1 green pepper, seeded and chopped
2 medium zucchini, thinly sliced
2 cups spinach pasta noodles
salt and pepper to taste
1/2 cup grated Parmesan

In hot skillet, brown sausage, then drain on paper towel. In stock pot, sauté onion and garlic in 3 tablespoons of sausage fat. Add tomatoes, breaking them apart. Add wine, broth, basil and oregano. Simmer, uncovered, for 30 minutes. Add parsley, green pepper, zucchini, noodles, salt and pepper and sausage. Simmer, covered, for 30 minutes. Serve in deep bowls passing Parmesan cheese separately. Additional water may be added if soup becomes too thick.

Cheddar Cheese and Vegetable Chowder

Serves 4-6

1 cup green pepper, chopped
1 cup potatoes, cubed
1/4 cup onion, chopped
1 cup carrots, chopped
4 tablespoons butter
5 tablespoons flour
2 10 3/4 oz. cans chicken broth
1 10 oz. package frozen peas
2 cups milk
3 cups grated cheddar cheese
salt and pepper to taste

In a saucepan, cook green pepper, potatoes, onion and carrots in water until tender. Drain water. In a separate pan begin the soup base. Melt butter, stir in flour and blend well. Add chicken broth and bring to a boil, stirring constantly. Add cooked vegetables, peas, milk and cheese. Cook on low heat until the cheese is melted. Do not boil after cheese is added. Salt and pepper to taste.

Vegetable Barley Soup

Serves 6

1 medium sized green pepper, chopped
1/2 cup onion, chopped
1 clove garlic, minced
2 tablespoons olive oil
1 large can tomatoes
1 teaspoon salt
1/2 teaspoon basil
1/2 teaspoon oregano
dash of thyme
3/4 cup quick barley or 1/2 cup
regular barley
4 1/2 cups water
2 cups broccoli pieces
3 carrots, cut julienne
1 cup celery slices
parsley (optional garnish)

Sauté green pepper, onion and garlic in olive oil. Add tomatoes, seasoning, barley and water. Simmer 10 minutes for quick cooking barley, 40 minutes for regular barley. Add broccoli, carrots and celery. Simmer for 30 minutes or until vegetables are tender. Garnish with parsley.

Red Onion Soup with Apple Cider
Serves 4

2 tablespoons butter
1 teaspoon minced garlic
1 1/2 lb. red onions, thinly sliced
2 teaspoons all purpose flour
3 cups beef stock or canned broth
3 cups chicken stock or canned broth
1/2 cup dry white wine or vermouth
1/2 cup apple cider
1 bay leaf
1 teaspoon dried thyme, crumbled
salt and pepper to taste
1 French baguette, sliced 1/2" thick
freshly grated Swiss cheese
or white cheddar

Melt butter in large saucepan. Add onion and garlic and cook until light golden brown, stirring frequently (about 20 minutes). Stir in flour. Add both stocks, wine, cider and bay leaf. Bring to boil, skimming surface occasionally. Add thyme, reduce heat and simmer 40 minutes. Season with salt and pepper. Preheat broiler. Place bread slices on baking sheet. Top with cheese. Broil until cheese melts. Ladle soup into bowls. Top with cheese bread croutons.

Sausage and Tortellini Soup
Serves 4

1/2 lb. Italian sausage
2 tablespoons canola oil
1 medium onion, chopped
3 cloves garlic, chopped
4 cups chicken broth or stock
16 oz. can chopped or crushed tomatoes
1/2 cup white wine
1 8 oz. can tomato sauce
1 zucchini, sliced
1 large carrot, sliced
2 teaspoons dried Italian seasoning
1 8-10 oz. package cheese tortellini
freshly grated Asiago cheese

In 3-quart saucepan or Dutch oven, cook sausage in 1 tablespoon oil until cooked through, 10-15 minutes. Drain on paper towel and set aside. Sauté onion and garlic in remaining oil until translucent. Add cooked sausage, broth, tomatoes, wine, tomato sauce, vegetables and seasonings to pot. Bring to a simmer over medium heat and cook, stirring occasionally, until vegetables are almost tender. Add tortellini to soup and cook until tortellini are cooked through. Season with salt and pepper, if desired. Serve topped with Asiago cheese.

Leek and Potato Soup
Serves 6-8

3 tablespoons butter
3 cups sliced leeks (white part only) or
onions, or combination of both
2 stalks celery, diced
2 tablespoons flour
1 quarts hot water
1 quart chicken broth
1 teaspoon salt
freshly ground pepper to taste
1 cup or so of tender green part
of the leeks, sliced
4 cups (about 1 1/2 lb.) potatoes,
peeled and diced
1 carrot, thinly sliced
chopped parsley (garnish)

Melt butter in 4-quart heavy-bottomed pan over medium heat. Stir in the leeks and/or onions and celery. Cover pan and cook slowly for 5 minutes without browning. Blend in the flour and stir constantly, over moderate heat, for 2 minutes. Do not allow mixture to brown. Remove from heat, let cool a bit and gradually blend in a cup of hot water. Add remaining water, chicken broth, salt, pepper, green leeks, potatoes and carrot. Bring to boil and simmer, for about 40 minutes, until vegetables are tender. Garnish with fresh parsley.

Cheesy Potato Soup
Serves 8

6 cups potatoes, peeled, diced
2 cups water
1 cup celery, chopped fine
1 cup carrots, grated
1/2 cup chopped onion
2 teaspoons parsley, chopped
2 chicken bouillon cubes
1 teaspoon salt
pepper to taste
3 cups milk mixed with
4 tablespoons flour
1 lb. Velveeta cheese cut into slices

Put first nine ingredients in a soup pot and cook until vegetables are tender. Then add milk and flour mixture. Cook until thickened. Melt cheese into soup and serve.

Minestrone Soup
Serves 8

1/4 lb. bacon
1/4 lb. ham
1/4 lb. Italian sausage
2 cloves garlic, minced
1 large onion, diced
1 zucchini, chopped
2 stalks celery, chopped
1 leek, chopped
1 tablespoon basil
salt and pepper
dash of allspice
2 quarts beef or chicken stock
1/2 cup canned kidney beans
2 cups cabbage, chopped
1/2 cup wine
1 large can tomatoes
1/2 cup elbow macaroni, cooked

Cook bacon until crisp. Drain off excess fat and set aside. Brown sausage and drain excess fat. Combine bacon, sausage, ham and garlic in large kettle. Add onions, zucchini, celery, leeks, basil, salt, pepper and allspice. Simmer for 10 minutes. Add stock, beans, cabbage and wine. Simmer 1 1/2 hours. Then add tomatoes and macaroni. Boil. Thin stock if necessary.

Chicken Chili
Serves 8

1/4 cup flour
1 1/2 teaspoon cumin
1 teaspoon white pepper
1 onion, chopped
3 cloves garlic, minced
2 tablespoons oil
3 cups chicken broth
1 4 oz. can diced chilies
2 cans white beans, drained
3 deboned chicken breasts,
cooked and cubed

Combine first three ingredients in bowl. Cook onion and garlic in oil. Add flour mixture. Add chicken broth, chilies and cook until thick. Add beans and chicken and heat through.

Kathy's Wonderful Chicken Noodle Soup
Serves 6-8

4 chicken breasts, cut into small pieces
6 cups water
4 chicken bouillon cubes
1 small can chicken broth
3/4 cup broccoli pieces
1 small onion, diced
2 stalks celery, diced
3/4 cup cabbage, cubed
4 medium potatoes, cubed
salt and pepper, to taste
1/2 cup Velveeta cheese
1/2 package egg noodles

Put first four ingredients in pan and simmer. Put broccoli, onion, celery, cabbage and potatoes in food processor with 1 cup water. Pulverize. Add this to chicken mixture and simmer two hours. Add salt and pepper to taste. Add cheese and egg noodles. Simmer until noodles are tender.

Sweet Potato Corn Chowder
Serves 8

3 oz. slab bacon, chopped
1 small onion, chopped
1/2 cup chopped sweet red pepper
1/2 cup chopped leek, white part only
1 teaspoon fresh or 1/4 teaspoon dried thyme
1 teaspoon chopped fresh or 1/4 teaspoon dried marjoram
1/2 teaspoon salt
1/4 teaspoon pepper
2 medium sized sweet potatoes, peeled and cut into 1/2" chunks
1 cup fresh or frozen corn
14 1/2 oz. can chicken broth
3 cups water
2 teaspoons cornstarch
1/2 cup heavy cream

In a heavy 4-quart saucepan, sauté bacon over medium heat until crisp. Remove bacon with a slotted spoon and drain on paper towels. Add onion, red pepper, leek, thyme, marjoram, salt and pepper to pan with bacon drippings. Sauté, stirring occasionally, for 10 minutes. Add sweet potatoes, corn, chicken broth and 2 1/2 cups water to mixture in saucepan. Cook until sweet potatoes are tender, 15 to 20 minutes. Mix cornstarch into remaining 1/2 cup water. Stir into soup mixture. Heat soup to boiling, stirring constantly, and cook until thickened. Reduce heat to low, stir in cream and reserved bacon. Heat just until bubbles appear at sides of pan. Serve immediately.

Cortez Aztec Soup
Serves 8

2 lb. boneless, skinless chicken breasts, cut into 1/2 inch strips
4 cups carrots, julienne
2 cups celery, sliced
1 cup green bell pepper, julienne
1 cup red pepper, julienne
1 cup onion, chopped
4 cloves garlic, minced
1 teaspoon oregano
1 teaspoon basil
1/2 teaspoon cumin
12 cups chicken broth
1 large tomato, seeded and chopped
4 tablespoons lime juice
5 bay leaves
1 teaspoon salt
1/2 teaspoon black pepper
3 tablespoons finely chopped cilantro
tortilla strips (purchased commercially)
1 1/2 cups Monterey Jack cheese, grated
1 avocado, peeled and chopped (optional garnish)

Sauté chicken breast strips until browned and no longer pink. Set aside. Sauté carrots, celery, pepper, onion, garlic, oregano, basil and cumin over medium heat for 5 minutes. Stir in chicken broth, chopped tomato, lime juice, bay leaves, salt and pepper. Heat to boil. Reduce heat and simmer for 15 to 20 minutes. Stir in cilantro. To serve, put some tortilla strips in bottom of each soup bowl. Sprinkle tortilla strips with Monterey jack cheese. Ladle soup over cheese and top with some chopped avocado.

French Market Soup
Serves 8

5 quarts water
3 cups dry mixed beans
Ham hocks
1 onion, chopped
1 small can tomatoes, diced
1/2 cup celery, diced
1 lb. country sausage link, sliced
1 cup red wine

Soak beans overnight. Simmer ham hocks and beans in water for several hours until beans are tender. Cut meat off ham hocks. Add onion, tomatoes and celery. Simmer one hour. Add wine and sausage. Simmer one more hour.
(More flavorful the second day.)

Chili a la Purifoy
Serves 10-12

2 lb. ground beef or turkey
2 cups chicken broth
2 onions, chopped
1 green pepper, chopped
2 15 oz. cans red kidney beans
4 teaspoons Worcestershire sauce
2 21 oz. cans diced tomatoes
2 teaspoons sugar
chili powder, to taste
chopped jalapeno peppers, to taste
2 tablespoons cooking oil
grated cheddar cheese (garnish)
chopped onions (garnish)

Sauté onions and green pepper in cooking oil. Brown meat and drain off excess fat. Combine meat, onion, green pepper and all other ingredients (except cheese) in large pot. Bring to boil, then decrease heat to low and simmer until desired thickness. Garnish bowl of chili with grated cheese and chopped raw onions.

Cincinnati-Style Chili
Serves 10

2 lb. ground beef round
1 1/2 lb. boneless pork butt, cubed
1 tablespoon oil
1 large red onion, chopped
1 jalapeno pepper, seeded and minced
2 cloves garlic, crushed
28 oz. can crushed tomatoes
12 oz. can beer
water
2 packages chili-seasoning mix
1/2 teaspoon ground allspice
1/2 teaspoon ground cinnamon
1 lb. bow tie-shaped pasta, cooked
1 1/2 cups shredded sharp
Cheddar cheese

Brown ground beef in large skillet. Set aside. Brown boneless pork cubes. Add to cooked beef. Cook onion, jalapeno pepper and garlic, in oil, about three minutes or until onion is tender. Combine meat, vegetables and remaining ingredients in large kettle. Heat to boiling. Reduce heat and simmer for 45 minutes. Serve meat sauce over pasta noodles. Sprinkle each serving with shredded cheese.

White Chili with Salsa Verde
Serves 6-8

Salsa Verde:
2 cups coarsely chopped fresh tomatillos
or 2 11 oz. cans tomatillos, drained
and chopped
1/2 cup onion, chopped
1/2 cup fresh cilantro or parsley,
chopped
1 pickled jalapeno pepper
1 clove garlic, minced
1/2 teaspoon lemon pepper
1/2 teaspoon dried oregano leaves
1/2 teaspoon garlic powder
2 - 3 tablespoons lime juice

Combine all ingredients. Mix well. Chill for at least 30 minutes to blend flavors.

White Chili:
2 1/2 cups water
1 teaspoon lemon pepper
1 teaspoon cumin seed
(or 1/4 teaspoon cumin powder)
1 1/2 lb. boneless, skinless chicken
(about 4 breasts)
1 tablespoon olive oil
1 garlic clove, minced
1 cup chopped onions
2 cans Green Giant Shoepeg
White Corn
2 4 oz. cans chopped green chilies
1 teaspoon ground cumin
2 - 3 tablespoons lime juice
2 15 oz. cans great Northern beans,
undrained
tortilla chips
Monterey Jack cheese, grated

In large saucepan, combine water, 1 teaspoon lemon pepper and cumin. Bring to a boil. Add chicken. Reduce heat to low; cover and simmer 20 minutes. Remove chicken. Cube and return to saucepan. Sauté garlic and onion in 1 tablespoon oil. Add garlic, onions, corn, chilies, cumin, lime juice and beans to saucepan. Bring to boil. Simmer for 10 minutes. Ladle soup over tortilla chips. Top with cheese and salsa verde.

Quick 'n Easy Texas Chili
Serves 3-4

1 lb. ground beef
1 can tomato soup
1 medium onion, chopped
1 1/2 - 2 tablespoons chili powder
1 1/4 - 1 1/2 teaspoons cumin
1 clove garlic, minced
1 can Ranch Style beans
salt and pepper to taste
1 can diced green chilies (optional)
onions, chopped (optional garnish)
grated cheese (optional garnish)

Brown meat, onion and garlic. Drain off fat. Add remaining ingredients and simmer over low heat for 30 to 45 minutes. Top with chopped onions and grated cheese if desired.

Southwest Stew
Serves 6-8

1 lb. lean ground beef
1 1/2 cups diced onions
5 garlic cloves, minced
28 oz. can diced tomatoes with juice
2 15 oz. cans kidney beans,
rinsed and drained
17 oz. can whole kernel corn, drained
1 cup picante sauce
3/4 cup water
1 teaspoon ground cumin
1/2 teaspoon black pepper
salt to taste

In a large saucepan, brown beef, onions and garlic. Drain excess fat. Add remaining ingredients and bring to a boil. Simmer, covered for at least 30 minutes.

Pork Stew with Mushrooms and Carrots
Serves 6-8

3 tablespoons vegetable oil
3 1/2 lb. boneless pork, trimmed of excess fat and cut into 2" pieces
1 large onion, chopped
2 ribs celery, chopped
1 bay leaf
4 cups chicken broth
4 cups water
8 large carrots, cut diagonally into 1" pieces
1 lb. mushrooms, sliced thin
1/4 cup butter
1/4 cup flour
1 cup cream (optional)
1 tablespoon lemon juice
salt and pepper to taste
1/2 cup minced fresh parsley

Heat oil in kettle until hot but not smoking. Pat the pork dry and brown in batches, transferring it to a large bowl. Pour off the fat from the kettle. Return the pork to the kettle with the onion, celery, bay leaf, broth and water. Simmer, uncovered, for 1 1/2 hours or until the pork is tender. Add carrots and simmer, covered, for 15 minutes. Transfer pork and carrots with tongs to a bowl. Strain the mixture and return the cooking liquid to the kettle. In heavy skillet, cook the mushrooms in the butter over moderate heat until most of the liquid from the mushrooms has evaporated. Sprinkle the mixture with the flour and cook over moderate heat, scraping up the brown bits, for 3 minutes. If used, stir in the cream, stirring until it combines well. Add mushroom mixture to the cooking liquid and simmer the sauce, stirring until it has thickened. Stir in the lemon juice, pork, carrots and add salt and pepper to taste. May be made 2 days in advance and kept covered and chilled. Stir in the parsley before serving. Serve over rice or noodles.

Winter Pork Stew
Serves 2

1 tablespoon butter
1 small onion, thinly sliced
1 clove garlic, minced
2 cups pork tenderloin cubes (or about 4
small boneless, skinless chicken thighs)
2 tablespoons flour
1 cinnamon stick
1 teaspoon curry powder
1/2 teaspoon ground ginger
5 crushed peppercorns
1 cup chicken broth
1 large sweet potato, peeled
and cut into 1" cubes
1 medium apple, cored and
cut into 1" cubes
1/4 cup golden raisins
salt to taste

Melt butter in large skillet. Add onions and garlic and sauté 2 minutes. Dust pork with flour and add to skillet. Brown pork on all sides (about 5 minutes). Add cinnamon stick, curry powder, ginger and peppercorns and sauté 1 minute. Add chicken broth and stir up browned bits in skillet. Add sweet potato and apple. Stir well. Cover and simmer until pork and potatoes are tender, about 20 minutes. Add raisins the last 5 minutes and simmer covered 5 minutes longer. Remove cinnamon stick. Season to taste with salt.

Dutch Oven Chicken Stew
Serves 4-6

2 lb. chicken thighs, skin removed
1 medium onion, diced
1 bell pepper, diced
3 cloves garlic, minced or 1/2 teaspoon
garlic powder
4 stalks celery, sliced
4 carrots, peeled, sliced
4 potatoes, scrubbed and
cut into large dice
water to cover
2 teaspoons instant chicken bouillon
1 tablespoon oregano
salt and pepper to taste

Brown chicken in hot Dutch oven. Add onion, bell pepper, garlic and celery. Cook 3 minutes. Add remaining vegetables and spices. Stir to mix and add water. Bring to boil. Cover and simmer for 45 minutes. Taste and adjust seasonings. Thicken if desired with flour and water or cornstarch and water.

Green Chilies
and Black Bean Stew
Serves 4-6

3 cans black beans or soak 3 cups black
beans for 24 hours
2 smoked ham hocks
2 onions, thinly sliced
2 small cans diced green chilies
1 small can diced jalapeno peppers
1 tablespoon cumin
4 lb. pork roast, cubed
14 oz. canned green chilies
(or roasted chilies), diced
1 cup flour
salt
2 cloves garlic, minced
10 oz. package frozen corn

Rinse beans. Place in large pot and cover
with cold water. Add ham hocks, onions,
chilies, jalapenos and cumin. Bring to boil
and then lower to a simmer. Cook until
beans are tender. Add salt to taste. Drain
excess water if necessary. Refrigerate.
Brown cubed pork in a large pot. Add flour
and brown. Add garlic and chilies. Cover
with water. Bring to a boil and simmer until
stew meat is tender and sauce is thick. Add
corn and black beans. Heat and serve.

Stew En Croute
Serves 4

4 cups chicken stock
8 white pearl onions, peeled
2 cups white potatoes, diced
2 carrots, cut in 1" pieces
3/4 cup peas
1 lb. sausage, cut into 1" pieces
3 tablespoons butter
4 1/2 tablespoons flour
1/2 cup cream
salt and pepper to taste
Pastry dough for two-crust pie

Heat stock in saucepan. Add onions; cook
2 minutes. Add potatoes, carrots and
sausage; cook 10 minutes. Add peas;
remove from heat. With slotted spoon,
transfer contents of saucepan to four 2 1/2-
cup bowls; reserve broth. In small saucepan,
melt butter and flour; cook 3 minutes.
Whisk in broth. Cook until sauce thickens
(2-3 minutes). Add cream. Cook 1 minute.
Season with salt and pepper. Pour over stew
in bowls. Roll out pastry; fit to top of each
bowl and crimp edges; cut vent in center.
Bake, in 425 degree oven, for 10 minutes.
Lower temperature to 350 degrees and bake
20-25 minutes.

Lamb Stew
Serves 4

2 tablespoons olive oil
2 lb. lamb pieces
2 yellow onions, chopped
8 cloves garlic, minced
2 cups vegetable stock or water
4 cups small white beans, cooked
3 carrots, peeled and cut into 1" pieces
3/4 teaspoon fresh rosemary
2 bay leaves
salt and pepper to taste
1 cup fine dried bread crumbs

Warm oil in heavy soup pot over medium high heat. Add lamb in batches and brown well on all sides, (about 5 minutes). Transfer to a dish and set aside. Add onions and garlic to the pot; sauté until browned (3-4 minutes). Add stock or water and bring to a simmer. Add reserved lamb, beans, carrots, rosemary and bay leaves. Cover and simmer gently until meat is tender when pierced with a fork; about 1 hour. Discard bay leaves. Season to taste with salt and pepper. Spoon into bowls. Top with bread crumbs and bake in 350 degree oven, for 5-10 minutes, until golden brown.

Brandied Peach Soup
Serves 4

29 oz. can peach halves in heavy syrup
1/2 teaspoon ground cinnamon
1/8 teaspoon ground white pepper
1 cup dry or sweet white wine
2 tablespoons cornstarch
1/2 cup water
1/2 cup sour cream
1 1/2 tablespoons brandy
1 tablespoon freshly squeezed lemon juice
sliced fresh or canned peaches (optional)

Drain peach halves, reserving 1 cup of the syrup. Puree peaches in food processor. Transfer to a medium-sized saucepan; add cinnamon, white pepper, wine and reserved syrup. In a 1-cup measure, blend cornstarch and water together; set aside. Bring peach mixture to a boil and whisk in cornstarch mixture. Cook 1 to 2 minutes, stirring constantly, until mixture thickens. In a small bowl, whisk sour cream, brandy and lemon juice together. Add to peach mixture. Pour soup into a container; refrigerate. Serve soup well chilled. Garnish with sour cream swirls or sliced peaches.

Miners at Daly Mine

Before 1912, a miner stabbed a dagger-like candle holder into the timber near his work. He used a daily supply of three candles for light during his ten-hour shift. Candles not only provided illumination, but served as a warning for insufficient oxygen and explosions. If the flame flickered, the miners dropped their tools and ran for the surface. Miners were able to escape some explosions, but even a healthy diet of salad greens would not have prevented the dreaded Miner's Con disease.

Szechwan Noodle Toss
Serves 6

1 tablespoon salt
3 tablespoons vegetable oil
8 oz. thin spaghetti
2 large red peppers, seeded,
cored and julienned
4 scallions, cut diagonally in 1" pieces
1 medium clove garlic, crushed
1 lb. spinach leaves, washed, drained
and cut in 1" pieces
3/4 lb. firm tofu or cooked
chicken, cubed
8 oz. can sliced water chestnuts, drained

Dressing:
3 tablespoons vegetable oil
1/4 cup low-sodium soy sauce
2 tablespoons dark sesame oil
2 tablespoons rice vinegar
1 1/2 teaspoons crushed
red pepper flakes

In a 5-quart saucepan, over high heat, bring 3 quarts water, salt and 1 tablespoon of the vegetable oil to a rolling boil. Add pasta, stirring to separate strands. Cover pan until water returns to boiling. Uncover and cook pasta 7 to 9 minutes or until pasta is al dente. Drain and rinse pasta thoroughly. Set aside. In large skillet, heat 2 tablespoons of the vegetable oil. Add red peppers, scallions and garlic. Sauté 2 minutes, stirring constantly with a wooden spoon until vegetables are crisp-tender. Add spinach to red pepper mixture. Cover and cook 1 minute. Gently transfer vegetable mixture to the reserved bowl of pasta. Add tofu (or chicken) and chestnuts. In a small bowl combine dressing ingredients. Pour dressing over salad and toss gently. Serve immediately or refrigerate and serve well chilled.

Sarah's Salad
Serves 4-6

2 cups torn iceberg lettuce
2 cups torn romaine lettuce
2 cups torn leaf lettuce
6 tablespoons mayonnaise
3 teaspoons sugar
1 medium onion, chopped
1 cup Swiss cheese, shredded
1 1/2 cup cooked peas
4-6 slices cooked crisp bacon, crumbled

Place one third of the greens in a bowl. Dot with 2 tablespoons mayonnaise. Sprinkle with 1 teaspoon sugar. Top with one third onion, cheese and peas. Repeat layers. Do not toss. Cover and chill two hours. Just before serving top with crumbled bacon and toss.

Peasant Salad
Serves 4

4 medium tomatoes
2 medium cucumbers
1 large yellow pepper
1 medium red onion
1/4 cup lightly packed chopped
fresh basil
2 tablespoons capers, drained

Dressing:
1 garlic clove, chopped fine
2/3 cup olive oil
1/4 cup red wine vinegar
1 1/2 teaspoons salt
1/4 teaspoon pepper

Cut vegetables into bite-sized pieces. Place in large bowl. Sprinkle basil and capers over cut-up vegetables. Mix dressing ingredients. Just before serving, toss vegetables with dressing.

Spicy Black Bean and Corn Salad
Serves 6-8

16 oz. can black beans,
rinsed and drained
4 oz. Monterey jack cheese, cubed
16 oz. can whole kernel corn, drained
1 bunch green onions, sliced with tops
3/4 cup thinly sliced celery
1 small red pepper, diced
3/4 cup mild picante sauce
2 tablespoons olive oil
2 tablespoons lemon juice
1 teaspoon ground cumin
1 clove garlic, minced

Combine beans, cheese, corn, green onions, celery and red pepper in large bowl. Separately combine picante sauce, oil, lemon juice, cumin and garlic. Mix well. Toss with bean mixture. Chill, if desired. Serve with additional picante sauce.

Bleu Cheese Lima Bean Salad
Serves 4

3 cans lima beans, drained
(or 1 lb. cooked)
1 medium tomato, diced
1 small onion, minced
4 oz. bleu cheese, crumbled

Dressing:
1/4 cup olive oil
2 tablespoons cider vinegar
1 tablespoon lemon juice
1/4 teaspoon salt
1/4 teaspoon pepper
1 teaspoon dried oregano
leaves, crumbled
1 teaspoon minced garlic (1 clove)

Whisk all dressing ingredients in large serving bowl until well blended. Add remaining ingredients and toss to mix and coat. Cover and refrigerate overnight or up to 2 days. Toss lightly before serving.

Two Bean Salad
Serves 4

1/4 cup olive oil
2 tablespoons fresh lemon juice
coarse black pepper to taste
1 1/2 cup canned black beans,
rinsed and drained
3 large plum tomatoes,
seeded and diced
4 ribs celery, sliced
6 large radishes, sliced
1 pound green beans, 1-inch pieces

In bowl whisk together oil, lemon juice, pepper and salt to taste. Add black beans, tomatoes, celery and radishes. Toss to combine. (Salad may be prepared up to this point 2 days ahead and kept chilled and covered.) In a 3-quart saucepan, cook beans in boiling salted water until just tender (about 5 minutes). Drain. Stir into bean mixture and serve at room temperature.

Grilled Potato Salad
Serves 4

2 lb. small red potatoes
1 tablespoon salt
7 slices bacon, cooked and crumbled
5 tablespoons vegetable oil
5 scallions, quartered lengthwise and cut
crosswise into inch pieces
2 tablespoons cider vinegar
coarse black pepper and salt to taste

In a large saucepan combine potatoes with cold water that covers the potatoes by 2 inches. Bring to a boil. Add salt and simmer, covered, until potatoes are just tender (about 10 to 15 minutes). Drain and cool. Halve potatoes and toss gently with 2 tablespoon oil to coat well. Arrange potatoes, cut side down on an oiled rack. Set rack 5 to 6 inches over glowing coals and grill until golden (about 4 to 5 minutes). In a large bowl toss potatoes with bacon, remaining 3 tablespoons of oil, vinegar, scallions, salt and pepper to taste. Serve at room temperature.

Marinated Fresh Tomatoes
Serves 4

3 medium tomatoes, sliced
1 green pepper, cut into rings (optional)
2 green onions, thinly slices
3 tablespoons tarragon vinegar
2 tablespoons sugar
6 tablespoons oil
1/2 teaspoon salt
1/2 teaspoon oregano
1/4 teaspoon crushed dried tarragon
1/8 teaspoon celery seed

Arrange first three ingredients in flat dish. Thoroughly blend remaining ingredients and pour over vegetables. Cover tightly with saran wrap. Refrigerate at least one hour before serving.

Tortellini Shrimp Salad
Serves 4

9 oz. package cheese filled tortellini
2 small zucchini, sliced
2 small tomatoes, cut into wedges
7 oz. can artichoke hearts, drained and
quartered
3 1/2 oz. can sliced ripe olives, drained
1 lb. cooked salad shrimp
1/2 cup chopped fresh basil
grated Parmesan cheese

Herb Dressing:
3/4 cup olive oil
1/4 cup red wine vinegar
2 cloves garlic, minced
1/4 teaspoon dried tarragon leaves
salt and pepper to taste

Cook tortellini as directed on package. Drain and cool. Mix together herb dressing ingredients. Gently toss all ingredients with dressing. Sprinkle with Parmesan cheese.

Red Cabbage Coleslaw
Serves 4

6 cups of sliced red cabbage
(about 1 lb.)
1 small red onion thinly sliced
1/2 cup sour cream
1/3 cup mayonnaise
3 tablespoons minced fresh dill
2 tablespoons fresh lemon juice

In large bowl combine cabbage and onion. In a small bowl mix together remaining ingredients and add to cabbage mixture, tossing well. Season coleslaw with salt and pepper and chill, covered for 1 hour. May be made one day ahead. Serve chilled or at room temperature.

Caesar Salad
Serves 6

1 large head romaine lettuce
1 clove garlic, halved
1/2 cup olive oil
1 cup French bread cubes, crusts removed
1/2 teaspoon salt
1/4 teaspoon dry mustard
1/4 teaspoon ground black pepper
1 1/2 teaspoons Worcestershire sauce
1 large egg
1/4 cup crumbled bleu cheese
2 tablespoons grated Parmesan cheese
2 tablespoons freshly squeezed lemon juice
6 whole anchovy fillets (optional)

Clean lettuce and tear into bite-size pieces. Place lettuce in plastic bag and chill for several hours or overnight. Several hours before serving, crush one half garlic clove and combine with olive oil in a jar. Cover and refrigerate at least one hour. Remove garlic. In skillet, heat 2 tablespoons garlic-flavored oil. Add bread cubes and sauté until brown all over. Set aside. To remaining garlic-flavored oil in jar, add salt, mustard, pepper, Worcestershire sauce. Shake vigorously. Refrigerate. In a small saucepan, pour water to a 2-inch depth and bring water to a boil. Turn off heat. Carefully lower egg into water and let stand for 1 minute. Lift out egg. Set aside to cool. Just before serving, rub inside of large wooden salad bowl with the other half of garlic clove. Discard garlic. Add lettuce to the bowl. Shake dressing well and pour over lettuce. Sprinkle with both kinds of cheese. Break coddled egg over center of salad. Pour lemon juice directly over egg. Toss well. Sprinkle with sautéed bread cubes and toss again. Garnish with whole anchovies and serve at once.

Green Bean and Feta Cheese Salad
Serves 4-6

1 lb. fresh green beans, end
and stems trimmed
1 red onion, julienne cut
1/4 lb. feta cheese
1/4 cup balsamic vinegar
or sweet vinegar
2 tablespoons fresh lemon juice
salt and pepper to taste

Blanch beans in boiling water for 4 minutes until tender crisp. Shock in cold water. Cut into bite-sized pieces. Sauté red onion until tender, about 5 minutes. Chunk feta cheese and mix with onion and beans. Mix balsamic vinegar and lemon juice. Sprinkle over salad and toss to mix well. Salt and pepper to taste. Better if made 1-2 hours ahead of serving.

Cabbage Patch Coleslaw
Serves 6

2 cups crisp shredded cabbage
1/2 cup chopped parsley
1/2 cup sliced green onions

Dressing:
2 to 3 tablespoons sugar
3 tablespoons cider vinegar
2 tablespoons salad oil
1 teaspoon salt

Combine vegetables. Blend dressing ingredients, stirring to dissolve sugar. Pour dressing over vegetables. Toss.

Pasta Salad with Spinach and Feta Cheese
Serves 8-10

12 oz. spinach fettuccine
6 tablespoons olive oil
1 lb. fresh spinach (or 10 oz. frozen leaf spinach, thawed)
1/2 lb. feta cheese, crumbled
12 cherry tomatoes, sliced in half
2 tablespoons fresh chopped basil
12 black olives, sliced in half

Vinaigrette dressing:
1/2 cup olive oil
1/4 cup vegetable oil
1/4 cup red wine vinegar
1 teaspoon Dijon mustard
1 clove garlic, minced
pinch of thyme
salt and pepper to taste

Cook pasta, drain and rinse with cold water. Toss pasta with 3 tablespoons of olive oil. Steam spinach, squeeze out water and chop into bite-size pieces. Add cheese, tomatoes and olives. Toss basil in remaining 3 tablespoons of oil. Add to salad and toss. Pour vinaigrette over salad and toss. (May not need all of the vinaigrette dressing.)

Eastern Pasta Salad
Serves 4-6

3/4 lb. dried pasta
dash of olive oil
14 oz. can chick peas, drained
4 tablespoons fresh mint
finely grated zest of 1 lemon

Dressing:
3 cloves crushed garlic
6 tablespoons extra virgin olive oil
3 tablespoons wine vinegar
freshly squeezed juice of 1 lemon
salt and pepper to taste

Bring a large pan of water to boil and add dash of olive oil and pasta. Cook for about 10 minutes, stirring occasionally until tender. Drain and rinse under cold water. Drain again and place in a large mixing bowl. Add chick peas, mint and lemon zest to the pasta. Mix dressing ingredients in a covered jar and shake well to mix. Pour the dressing over the pasta mixture and mix well to combine. Cover and chill for 30 minutes. Toss before serving.

Taco Salad Bowl
Serves 8

1 1/2 lb. ground beef chuck or ground turkey
2 cloves garlic
4 oz. can mild green chilies, finely chopped and drained
1 lb. canned whole, peeled tomatoes packed in juice, undrained
2 teaspoons chili powder
1 teaspoon salt
1/8 teaspoon pepper
8 cups lettuce (iceberg, Boston, leaf or romaine), torn in bite-sized pieces
6 oz. Cheddar cheese, shredded
2 medium-sized tomatoes, diced
1 bunch scallions with green tops, chopped
7 oz. package tortilla chips or corn chips
black olives, sliced
sour cream

Brown meat and garlic in skillet until meat is browned. Drain off fat. Return to heat and add chilies, tomatoes, chili powder, salt and pepper. Mix well and cook over low heat, uncovered, for about 30 minutes or until most of moisture has evaporated. Just before serving, place lettuce in a large chilled bowl. Arrange tortilla chips around outer edge. Top lettuce with meat mixture, cheese scallions, chopped tomato and sliced olives. Top with dollop of sour cream. Toss just before serving.

Tenderloin Spinach Salad
Serves 2-3

8 oz. tenderloin, sliced thin
2 tablespoons butter
1 tablespoon Worcestershire sauce
1 teaspoon garlic salt (or to taste)
2 tablespoons green onion, chopped
1/4 cup sliced fresh mushrooms
2 tablespoons Parmesan cheese
3-4 cups fresh spinach (or mixed greens)
1/4 cup sliced black olives
bleu cheese dressing, to taste
chopped parsley (optional garnish)

Sauté tenderloin in butter. Add Worcestershire, garlic salt, onions, mushrooms and Parmesan cheese and cook until meat is medium rare. Cool to room temperature. Serve on a bed of greens. Sprinkle with black olives. Top with bleu cheese dressing. Garnish with parsley and Parmesan.

Curry Chicken Salad

Serves 4

two whole chicken breasts
white wine
1/2 head butter lettuce
1/2 head curly lettuce

Dressing:
1 cup mayonnaise
2 tablespoons soft cream cheese
1/2 cup chutney
1/2 teaspoon ground cinnamon
1/4 teaspoon curry (add to taste)

croutons (optional)
mandarin oranges (optional)
slivered almonds (optional)

Boil chicken in white wine. Simmer 6 to 7 minutes. Let sit 5 to 10 minutes. Drain. Cut chicken into bite-sized pieces. Prepare lettuce. Mix dressing ingredients. Toss together chicken, lettuce and enough dressing for personal preference. Add croutons, mandarin oranges, or almonds if desired.

Salsa Chicken Salad

Serves 4-6

2 eggs
3 tablespoons salsa
1/4 teaspoon salt
1 cup bread crumbs
1 teaspoon chili powder
1 teaspoon ground cumin
3/4 teaspoon garlic powder
1/4 teaspoon oregano
4-6 chicken breasts
lettuce

Garnishes: chopped avocado, chopped green onions, cherry tomatoes, lime wedges, salsa, sour cream

Coat baking dish with either spray oil or melt 1/4 cup of butter in oven. Mix together eggs, salsa and salt. Set aside. Mix together bread crumbs, chili powder, cumin, garlic powder and oregano. Dip chicken in egg mixture and roll in crumb mix. Place in prepared baking dish. Bake, at 350 degrees, for 25 minutes. Serve chicken on a bed of lettuce with assorted garnishes.

Grilled Chicken and Mandarin Orange Salad
Serves 6

6 medium chicken breast, skin and bones removed
1 head green leaf lettuce
1 head red leaf lettuce
3 stalks celery, finely chopped
3 large green onions, sliced including tops
15 oz. can mandarin oranges, drained, reserve 1/4 cup liquid for dressing
3/4 cup sugar
1 cup slivered almonds

Dressing:
1/4 cup apple cider vinegar
1/4 cup salad oil
1/4 cup sugar
10 dashes Louisiana style hot sauce
1/4 cup juice from mandarin oranges

Roll chicken breasts in salt and pepper. Grill. Set aside. Wash and tear lettuce and place in large bowl. Add celery, green onion and drained oranges. Chill. In large skillet, place sugar and almonds in medium to medium high heat. Melt sugar while stirring constantly with wooden spoon. Sugar will liquefy and turn a caramel color while coating almonds. Be careful not to burn sugar for this will ruin dish. When sugar has completely caramelized and coated the almonds, remove from heat and place on a plate to cool. Shake together vigorously all dressing ingredients until thickened and toss into large bowl with chilled greens. Divide evenly into six portions on large dinner plates. Top with candied almonds and sliced grilled chicken.

Grapefruit and Shrimp Salad
Serves 4

1 green onion
1 1/2 lb. jumbo shrimp, shelled,
deveined and cooked
1 pink grapefruit
1 head Boston lettuce
1 small head radicchio
1 cup Chicory pieces
1/2 cup sliced celery

Grapefruit Vinaigrette:
1/4 cup olive oil
3 tablespoons grapefruit juice
1 1/2 tablespoons cider vinegar
1 teaspoon Dijon mustard
1/2 teaspoon sugar
1/4 teaspoon dried oregano leaves,
crumbled

Cut green onion lengthwise into thin strips. Cut strips across into inch lengths. Drop in a small bowl of ice water. Cover and refrigerate 1 hour. In a medium size bowl, combine shrimp and grapefruit sections. Combine vinaigrette ingredients and shake well until combined. Add 2 tablespoons of vinaigrette to shrimp mixture. Toss well. Cover shrimp mixture with remaining vinaigrette and refrigerate for 1 hour. When ready to serve, tear Boston lettuce and radicchio into bite sized pieces. Drain green onion curls. In a large bowl toss together onion curls, chicory, lettuce, radicchio and celery. Add shrimp mixture. Toss once. Serve with remaining vinaigrette and a loaf of good crusty bread.

Bob Boyer's Secret Caesar Salad Dressing
Yield: 1 cup

2/3 cup olive oil
1/4 cup wine vinegar
juice of one medium lemon
couple dashes of Worcestershire
1 egg
2 cloves garlic
fresh ground pepper to taste
1/2 cup Parmesan cheese
1 teaspoon Dijon mustard

Mix in blender. For thicker dressing add another egg prior to serving. Blend well. Add anchovies to blender mix or add fresh shrimp to salad.

Homer's Salad Dressing
Yield: 1 cup

8 cloves garlic, crushed
1/4 cup white vinegar
2 teaspoons Bon Appetit
1 tablespoon oregano
1/2 cup extra virgin olive oil
1/2 cup tomato-basil feta cheese,
crumbled

Combine all ingredients in suitable container, except for cheese. Shake until well mixed. Add crumbled feta cheese. Shake again.

Poppy Seed Dressing
Yield: 3 cups

2 cups Wesson oil
1 1/2 cup sugar
2/3 cup red wine vinegar
3 tablespoons Dijon mustard
2 teaspoons salt
2 tablespoons poppy seeds

Mix first 5 ingredients in blender. Remove and stir in the poppy seeds.

French Dressing
Yield: 3 cups

1/2 cup sugar (scant)
2 teaspoons salt
2 teaspoons dry mustard
2 teaspoons paprika
1 teaspoon Worcestershire sauce
1/2 cup vinegar
1 cup oil
1 can tomato soup
1 small onion, peeled and sliced in half

Mix first eight ingredients with rotary beater. Marinate onion in dressing.

BREAKFASTS

The Miners

In the early 1900's, mining companies had boarding houses and family-style dining. Butchers were hired to cut meat and make sausages and bakers kept up a supply of breads. After breakfast, miners filled their own lunch buckets everyday from a buffet table of food. At the end of the day the miners returned their numbered lunch pails to be washed before their next shift.

Baked French Toast
with Berries
Serves 8

small loaf of day old French bread
3 eggs
3 tablespoons sugar
1 teaspoon vanilla extract
2 1/4 cup milk
1/2 cup all purpose flour
6 tablespoons dark brown sugar, packed
3/4 teaspoon ground cinnamon
1/4 cup butter or margarine
1 cup blueberries, fresh or frozen
1 cup strawberries, fresh or frozen

Diagonally cut bread into 1-inch slices and place in a well-greased 9" x 13" baking dish. In a medium bowl, lightly beat eggs, sugar and vanilla. Stir in the milk until well blended. Pour over bread, turning pieces to coat well. Cover and refrigerate overnight. Preheat oven to 375 degrees. In a small bowl, combine the flour, brown sugar and cinnamon. Cut in butter until mixture resembles coarse crumbs. Turn bread over in baking dish. Scatter blueberries over bread. Sprinkle evenly with crumb mixture. Bake about 40 minutes until golden brown. Cut into squares. Top with strawberries or serve them on the side.

Muesli
Serves 4

1/2 cup raisins
1/2 cup old fashioned oats
1 1/2 cup quick oats
1/3 cup brown sugar
1/4 - 1/2 teaspoon cinnamon
2 cups milk

fresh fruit

Combine first six ingredients. Cover and let sit overnight in the refrigerator. Add fresh fruit when you are ready to serve.

Crab Strata
Serves 6-8

2 tablespoons bread crumbs
8 slices white bread
1/2 lb. mushrooms, sliced
1/4 cup sliced green onions
1/4 cup Madeira
8 oz. crab meat
2 1/2 cups milk
4 eggs
2 cups shredded Cheddar cheese
1/2 teaspoon salt
1/2 teaspoon dry mustard
freshly ground pepper to taste

Butter a 2-quart soufflé dish or 6" x 10" baking dish and dust with bread crumbs. Set aside. Remove crusts from bread and cut bread into cubes. Set aside. In skillet, sauté mushrooms and onions in Madeira over medium heat. Stir in crab meat. In prepared soufflé dish, alternate layers of bread cubes and crab mixture, ending with bread cubes. In food processor or blender, whirl milk, eggs, cheese, salt, mustard and pepper until thoroughly blended. Slowly pour this mixture over bread cubes. Cover and refrigerate overnight. Bake, uncovered, at 325 degrees for 1 hour 30 minutes if using soufflé dish or 1 hour if using 6" x 10" dish. Strata is done when knife inserted in the center comes out clean.

Impossible Quiche Greek Style
Serves 8

4 eggs
1/2 cup Bisquick
1 1/2 cup milk
6 tablespoons butter, melted
salt and pepper, to taste
1/2 cup fresh spinach, steamed
1/4 cup feta cheese
1/2 cup diced tomatoes
1/4 cup Greek olives, sliced

Whip eggs, Bisquick, milk, butter, salt and pepper in blender. Pour into 9" pie plate. Sprinkle spinach, cheese, tomatoes and olives evenly onto mixture. Bake, at 350 degrees, for 45 minutes. The dish will form its own top and bottom crusts during the baking process. Impossible!

Stuffed French Toast Strata
Serves 6-8

1 lb. loaf unsliced French bread
8 oz. package cream cheese, cubed
8 eggs
2 1/2 cups milk, light cream or
half & half
6 tablespoons butter or
margarine, melted
1/4 cup maple syrup

Cut French bread loaf into cubes. You should have about 12 cups bread cubes. Grease a 13" x 9" x 2" inch baking dish. To assemble, place half of the bread cubes in the bottom of the prepared dish. Top with the cream cheese cubes, and then with the remaining bread cubes. In a blender container, or a mixing bowl with a rotary beater, mix together eggs, milk, melted butter or margarine and maple syrup until well blended. Pour egg mixture evenly over bread and cheese cubes. Using spatula, slightly press layers down to moisten. Cover with plastic wrap and refrigerate for 2 to 24 hours. Remove plastic wrap from baking dish. Bake, in a 325 degree oven, for 35 to 40 minutes, or until the center appears set and the edges are lightly golden. Let stand about 10 minutes before serving.

Up Country Sausage
Serves 6

1 lb. fresh pork sausage links
6 medium cooking apples, cored and
each cut into 8 wedges (2 lb. total)
3 tablespoons brown sugar
1 tablespoon lemon juice
1/4 teaspoon salt
1/8 teaspoon pepper

In a large 12-inch skillet, cook sausage over medium heat about 10 minutes or until no longer pink. Drain and discard juices. Cut sausage links crosswise in half. Return sausage links to the skillet. Add apple wedges. Then sprinkle with brown sugar, lemon juice, salt and pepper. Cover and cook over medium-low heat for 10 to 15 minutes or until apples are just tender, gently stirring once or twice.

Eggs Benedict
Serves 4

4 English muffins, toasted
8 eggs
8 thin tomato slices
8 thinly sliced slabs of Canadian Bacon
No Fail Hollandaise Sauce
(see directions below)
paprika

Prepare Hollandaise sauce. Set aside. Toast English muffins, butter lightly. Place muffins open-faced on four dinner plates, two halves on each plate. Warm Canadian Bacon slightly in fry pan. (Overcooked bacon will get tough.) Stack one slice on each English muffin half. Slice fresh tomatoes thinly and layer on top of Canadian bacon. Poach 8 eggs. If you don't have a poacher, you can carefully drop eggs into calmly boiling water and cook three minutes, then remove carefully with a slotted spoon. Place poached eggs on top of tomato slices. Top with No Fail Hollandaise Sauce, about two tablespoons per serving. Sprinkle with mild paprika to decorate.

No Fail Hollandaise Sauce

1 1/2 tablespoons white wine vinegar
1 1/2 tablespoons water
3 egg yolks
3 sticks butter, softened to
room temperature
lemon juice to taste

In double boiler, place vinegar and water. Over heat, reduce mixture to 1/4 its volume. Leaving bottom part of double boiler on the stove, remove from heat and add an extra 1 tablespoon cold water and egg yolks. Return mixture to heat over hot water in double boiler. Beat yolks with wire whisk until thick and lemony yellow. Cut butter into quarters. Add one piece butter at a time to egg mixture, stirring constantly with whisk, until completely incorporated. When all butter is added, remove from stove and continue stirring until cooled slightly. Add fresh lemon juice to taste.

Plum Streusel Coffee Cake
Serves 8

For streusel:
1 cup all purpose flour
1/2 cup firmly packed light brown sugar
2/3 cup walnuts
6 tablespoons unsalted butter, cut into pieces and softened
1 teaspoon cinnamon
1/3 teaspoon freshly grated nutmeg

Cake batter:
1/2 cup unsalted butter, softened
3/4 cup sugar
2 large eggs
1 1/4 teaspoon vanilla
1 1/4 cup all purpose flour
1 teaspoon baking powder
1/2 teaspoon salt
3/4 lb. plums (4 to 5 medium), sliced
confectioners' sugar for sifting over cake

Preheat oven to 350 degrees. Butter and flour a 9-inch round or square baking pan at least 2 inches deep. Make streusel in a food processor. Pulse all ingredients until combined well and crumbly. Make cake batter with an electric beater. Cream together butter and sugar until light and fluffy. Add eggs, one at a time, beating well after each addition. Add vanilla. Sift flour with baking powder and salt. Add to creamed mixture and beat until just combined. Spread cake batter in pan, smoothing top and arrange plum slices over it in slightly overlapping concentric circles. Sprinkle streusel over plum slices and bake cake in middle of oven for 1 hour, or until tester comes out clean. Cool cake slightly on a rack and sift confectioners' sugar over it. Serve warm or at room temperature.

Caramel Rolls for Breakfast
Yield: 12 rolls

3/4 cup butter, melted
1/4 cup light corn syrup
1 cup brown sugar
1/2 teaspoon cinnamon
1/2 cup chopped pecans
12 frozen white dinner rolls

Sprinkle 1/2 cup melted butter, corn syrup, brown sugar and cinnamon into greased bundt pan. Dip frozen rolls in remaining 1/4 cup melted butter. Arrange over other ingredients in bundt pan. Cover lightly and thaw overnight. In the morning, bake at 375 degrees for 30 minutes. Release Caramel Rolls from bundt pan onto pretty plate.

Apple Pancakes
Serves 4

1 cup all purpose flour
3 tablespoons confectioners' sugar
1 teaspoon baking powder
1/2 teaspoon salt
3 eggs
1 tablespoon vegetable oil
1 cup milk
2 cooking apples
2 tablespoons lemon juice
4 tablespoons butter or margarine
1/3 teaspoon ground cinnamon
2 tablespoons sugar
1/3 cup ground walnuts
sour cream

Sift flour, sugar, baking powder and salt into a medium-sized bowl. Beat eggs and oil into milk; stir into flour mixture. Chill 1 hour. While batter chills, pare and thinly slice apples, toss with lemon juice. Melt 1 tablespoon of butter, in a 7-inch skillet, over medium heat. Pour about 1/4 batter into pan, tilting to cover the bottom completely. Drain apples; arrange about 6 slices in batter. Cook until top is set and underside is golden; turn over and cook lightly on other side. Remove to plate; keep warm in low oven (200 degrees) while cooking remaining pancakes. Add butter to pan as needed. Combine cinnamon, sugar and nuts in small bowl. Fold pancakes in half; sprinkle with nut mixture. Serve with sour cream.

Oatmeal Pancakes
Yield: 18 pancakes

2 cups oatmeal
2 cups buttermilk
2 eggs, lightly beaten
1/2 cup melted butter
1/2 cup flour
2 tablespoons sugar
1 teaspoon baking powder
1 teaspoon baking soda
1/2 teaspoon cinnamon
1/4 teaspoon salt
1/2 cup raisins (optional)

Combine oatmeal and buttermilk. Refrigerate overnight. In the morning, add eggs and butter. In a small bowl combine all dry ingredients. Add to oatmeal mixture. Stir until moistened. If batter seems too thick, thin with a little buttermilk. Cook on lightly greased griddle.

Apple Butter
Yield: 6 cups

cooked apples
(use 1 cup apples to 3/4 cup sugar)
2 tablespoons cinnamon
1 1/2 tablespoons cloves
2 tablespoons allspice

Measure 6 cups of applesauce. Add spices. Put into large roaster and bake at 350 degrees for 1 hour or until thick. May use pears instead of apples.

Overnight Waffles with Dutch Honey
Serves 8

2 1/2 cups warm water
1 package active dry yeast
1 teaspoon sugar
2/3 cup low-fat dry milk
1/3 cup salad oil
1/2 teaspoon baking soda
1/2 teaspoon salt
2 large eggs
3 cups flour

In a large bowl combine water, yeast and sugar. Let stand 5 minutes. Add dry milk, oil, soda, salt, egg and flour. Beat until smooth. Bake in a waffle iron and serve with Dutch Honey. (This batter keeps for several days.)

For Dutch Honey, combine ingredients over medium heat and stir until boiling.

Dutch Honey:
1 cup sugar
1 cup whipping cream
1 cup maple syrup

Finnish Breakfast Rice
Serves 4

1 cup rice
6 cups whole milk
6 tablespoons butter
1 teaspoon salt
raisins, cinnamon and sugar (to taste)

Mix together rice, milk, butter and salt in a crock pot. Cook on low overnight. Serve warm with raisins, cinnamon and sugar. Refrigerate any leftovers. Can be reheated in microwave.

Make Ahead Breakfast Cake
Serves 6-8

1 1/4 cup flour
1/4 cup sugar
1 tablespoon baking powder
pinch of salt
1/4 cup shortening
2/3 cup milk
1 egg, lightly beaten

Topping:
4 tablespoons flour
6 tablespoons brown sugar
1/2 teaspoon cinnamon
3 tablespoons butter

Sift together flour, sugar, baking powder and salt. Cut shortening into dry ingredients. Add milk and egg. Pour into greased 8-inch square pan. Mix dry topping ingredients together. Cut butter into dry ingredients until well combined. Sprinkle topping over batter. Can be baked now or covered and refrigerated overnight. Bake at 400 degrees for 25 minutes.

Baked Apple Doughnuts
Yield: 6 dozen

3 cups all purpose flour
3 1/2 teaspoon baking powder
1 cup sugar
1 teaspoon salt
1 teaspoon nutmeg
1 cup shortening
2 eggs, beaten
1/2 cup milk
1 cup grated tart apples
1/2 cup chopped nuts
1/2 cup butter, melted
cinnamon and sugar mixture

Sift together flour, baking powder, sugar, salt and nutmeg. Cut in shortening until mixture is fine. Add eggs, milk, apples and nuts. Mix thoroughly. Fill tiny muffin tins about 2/3 full. Bake, at 350 degrees, for 20 to 25 minutes or until golden brown. Roll in melted butter, then cinnamon-sugar mixture.

Special California Coffee Cake
Serves 9-12

2 1/2 cups flour
1 cup brown sugar
3/4 cup white sugar
1 teaspoon baking powder
1 teaspoon baking soda
1/2 teaspoon salt
1 teaspoon cinnamon
1 teaspoon nutmeg
2 eggs, beaten
3/4 cup canola oil
1 cup buttermilk

Topping:
3/4 cup brown sugar
1 tablespoon flour
3 tablespoons butter, softened
1/2 teaspoon cinnamon
3/4 cup chopped walnuts

Sift together dry ingredients. Add beaten eggs, oil and buttermilk. Beat well. Pour into a greased 9" x 13" pan. Crumble together topping ingredients. Sprinkle on top of cake batter. Cut through with knife. Bake, at 350 degrees, for 45 minutes.

Miner's Hospital

Just as bread offers sustenance to ones diet the
local miners union gave support to building a
hospital in 1904. Funds for the Miner's Hospital
were raised through the efforts of the Western
Federation of Miners and shares purchased by
individual local miners at $25 each. There was a
critical need to provide local care for injured
miners, particularly those who suffered from
"Miner's Con" (miner's consumption) or silicosis,
a lung disease caused by inhaling rock dust while
drilling in the mines. The Hospital was originally
located near today's Resort Center. Later, through
community efforts, the building was relocated to the
City Park, renovated and used as a library.
The building now serves as a community center.

Bread Sticks
Yield: 20

2 packages active dry yeast
1 tablespoon granulated sugar
2 teaspoons salt
1/4 cup olive oil
1 1/2 cups warm water (110 degrees)
3-3 1/2 cups all-purpose flour
1 egg white beaten with
1 tablespoon water
coarse salt (optional)

In a large mixing bowl, combine yeast, sugar and salt. Add the oil and 1/4 cup water. Beat this mixture well with a wooden spoon for about 3 minutes. Add 1/2 cup flour and continue beating with the wooden spoon. Alternately add flour, 1 cup at a time, and water until you have a fairly soft dough. Knead dough, on well-floured surface, until it springs back and is smooth and satiny. Let the dough rest, covered with a towel, for about 5 minutes. Shape dough into a roll about 20 inches long. With a sharp knife cut the dough into 1-inch pieces. Rest the dough for 5 minutes and then roll the 1-inch pieces into desired lengths. Arrange bread sticks, 1-inch apart on slightly greased baking sheet. Let rest for 20 minutes and brush with egg and water mixture. Sprinkle with salt, if desired. Bake, at 300 degrees, for 30 minutes. Should be crisp and golden brown.

Blueberry Muffins
Yield: 12 large muffins

1 cup all purpose flour
2 teaspoons baking powder
1/2 teaspoon ground nutmeg
1/2 teaspoon salt
3/4 cup quick cooking oatmeal
1/2 cup firmly packed light brown sugar
1 egg
1 cup milk
1/4 cup vegetable oil
1 1/2 cup frozen blueberries, thawed

Sift flour, baking powder, nutmeg and salt into a medium bowl; stir in brown sugar and oatmeal until well blended. Beat egg in a 2-cup measure with a fork. Add and beat in milk and oil. Pour over dry ingredients and stir until just blended. Fold in blueberries. Grease 12 large muffin pan cups and spoon in batter dividing evenly. Bake, at 400 degrees, for 20 minutes or until golden brown. Cool in pan on wire rack for 5 minutes.

Herbed Popovers
Serves 6

1 cup all purpose flour
1/4 teaspoon salt
2 large eggs
1 cup milk
1 teaspoon fresh thyme, finely chopped
(or 1/4 teaspoon dried)
1 tablespoon unsalted butter, melted
2 tablespoons unsalted butter

Preheat oven to 450 degrees. Combine flour, salt, eggs, milk, thyme and melted butter. Beat with a wooden spoon until the mixture is the consistency of heavy cream. Divide the remaining 2 tablespoons of butter into 6 pieces and place 1 piece in each cup of popover pan. Place pan in oven for 1 minute until butter is bubbly. Fill each cup half full with batter and bake for 20 minutes. Reduce heat to 350 degrees and continue baking for an additional 15 to 20 minutes. Serve immediately.

Yorkshire Pudding Popovers
Serves 6

3 large eggs
1 cup milk
3 tablespoons butter or margarine
1 cup all purpose flour
2/3 teaspoon salt

Preheat oven to 400 degrees. Using butter, lightly but thoroughly grease the inside of six (6 oz. size) glass custard cups. Set cups aside while you prepare batter. In a medium bowl, mix together eggs, milk and butter with a whisk until thoroughly combined. Sift flour and salt over egg mixture. Continue beating batter until it is very smooth and no lumps remain. Pour batter into prepared custard cups, filling each about half full. Bake on a large jelly-roll pan 45 to 50 minutes or until deep golden brown. Serve hot.

Pumpkin-Nut Bread
Yield: 1 loaf

2 cups all-purpose flour
2 teaspoons baking powder
1/2 teaspoon salt
3/4 teaspoon pumpkin pie spice
1/4 teaspoon baking soda
1 cup packed brown sugar
1/3 cup shortening
2 eggs
1 cup canned pumpkin
1/4 cup milk
1/2 cup chopped walnuts

Grease bottom of loaf pan with shortening. Heat oven to 350 degrees. In a small bowl sift together flour, baking powder, salt, pumpkin pie spice and soda. In medium bowl, cream together brown sugar and shortening. Add one egg and beat well. Add the other egg and beat well. With wooden spoon, stir in pumpkin and milk. Stir in flour mixture just until smooth. Do not stir too much. Stir in nuts. Spread evenly in greased pan, scraping bowl with rubber scraper. Bake for 1 hour. Cool for 10 minutes. Remove bread from pan and cool completely on rack.

Cranberry Orange Bread
Yield: 1 loaf

1 cup sugar
1/4 cup vegetable shortening·
1 egg
2 cups all purpose flour
1 1/2 teaspoons baking powder
1/2 teaspoon baking soda
1/2 teaspoon salt
2 large naval oranges
1/2 cups chopped walnuts
1 cup fresh or frozen cranberries

Beat sugar and shortening in large bowl or electric mixer at high speed until fluffy. Beat in egg. Sift flour, baking powder, baking soda and salt together onto waxed paper. Grate rind (orange part only). Squeeze juice into a 2-cup measure. Add enough hot water to measure 1 1/4 cups liquid. Add dry ingredients to creamed mixture, mixing well. Stir in grated rind and juice mixture, then the nuts. Stir in cranberries. Pour into greased and floured 6-cup fluted pan or loaf pan. Bake in moderate oven (350 degrees) 50 minutes or until cake springs back when lightly touched with fingertip. Garnish with julienne strips of orange rind and cream cheese balls rolled in nuts, if you wish.

Country Nut Bread
Yield: 1 loaf

2 1/2 cups chopped dates
1 cup sweet Sherry
2 cups all purpose flour
1 teaspoon baking powder
1 teaspoon baking soda
1/4 teaspoon salt
1/4 cup butter flavored
vegetable shortening
1 cup firmly packed light brown sugar
1 egg
1/2 cup chopped candied cherries
1/2 cup walnuts

Combine dates and Sherry in a medium saucepan; heat slowly to bubbling; remove saucepan from heat; let stand 30 minutes. Sift flour, baking powder, baking soda and salt onto waxed paper. Beat shortening and brown sugar in medium bowl with electric mixer on high speed; beat in egg until creamy. Add sifted dry ingredients, alternately with Sherry-date mixture, stirring with wooden spoon, just until blended. Stir in red cherries and walnuts. Grease one 9"x5"x3" loaf pan. Add batter and smooth top. Bake in moderate oven (350 degrees) for 55 minutes or until wooden skewer inserted into center comes out clean. Cool in pan on wire rack for 10 minutes. Loosen loaf around edges of pan and invert onto wire rack. Cool completely. Wrap in plastic and let stand at room temperature two days before slicing.

Honey Wheat Muffins
Yield: 12 large muffins

1 1/2 cups all purpose flour
1 teaspoon baking soda
1 teaspoon baking powder
1/2 teaspoon ground mace
1/2 teaspoon salt
1 cup whole wheat flour
1 egg
1 cup milk
1/2 cup molasses
1/4 cup butter flavored shortening
1/2 cup raisins (optional)

Sift flour, baking soda, baking powder, mace and salt into a medium bowl; stir in whole wheat flour until well blended. Beat egg in a 4-cup glass measure with a fork. Beat in milk, molasses and shortening. Pour over dry ingredients. Stir just to blend; add raisins. Grease 12 large muffin pan cups and spoon in batter, dividing evenly. Bake, at 400 degrees, for 15 minutes or until golden brown. Cool in pan on wire rack for 5 minutes. Loosen muffins around cups with a sharp knife. Serve warm.

Walnut Zucchini Bread
Yield: 1 loaf

2 1/2 cups unsifted all-purpose flour
1 1/2 teaspoons ground cinnamon
1/2 teaspoon ground cloves
2 teaspoons baking soda
2 teaspoons baking powder
1 teaspoon salt
1 1/2 cups granulated sugar
3/4 cups vegetable oil
3 large eggs
2 cups grated unpeeled zucchini (1 lb.)
1 1/2 cup finely chopped walnuts
1 teaspoon vanilla extract
1/4 cup confectioners' sugar (optional)
10 walnut halves (optional)

Preheat oven to 350 degrees. Using solid vegetable shortening, thoroughly grease the inside of a 9"x 5"x 3" loaf pan; set aside. On a sheet of waxed paper, sift together the flour, cinnamon, cloves, baking soda, baking powder and salt. Set aside. In large bowl of electric mixer, at medium speed, beat 1 1/2 cups granulated sugar, the vegetable oil and the eggs until smooth. Remove bowl from electric mixer (or beat sugar mixture with a wooden spoon). Using a wooden spoon, gradually stir sifted dry ingredients into sugar mixture, until smooth and no traces of flour remain. Add zucchini, chopped walnuts and vanilla; stir gently with wooden spoon until ingredients are thoroughly combined. Gently pour zucchini bread batter into the prepared loaf pan. Place on center rack in oven and bake for 1 hour and 15 minutes or until a cake tester inserted into center of bread comes out clean. Remove pan from oven; let cool 10 minutes. Remove bread from pan; place on wire rack to cool completely. (This cooling process can take several hours.) If desired, wrap cooled bread in aluminum foil and store in the refrigerator for up to 2 days. Return bread to room temperature before garnishing. Turn bread over and place bottom side up on a board; cover center and sides with strips of foil; sift confectioners' sugar along edges. Remove foil and decorate the center with walnuts. To serve, cut into thin slices.

Banana-Bran Bread
Yield: 1 loaf

1 1/2 cups sifted all-purpose flour
2 teaspoons baking powder
2/3 teaspoon baking soda
1/2 teaspoon salt
1/4 cup butter or margarine, softened
2/3 cup sugar
1 large egg
1 teaspoon vanilla extract
4 small fully ripe bananas
1 cup whole bran cereal
2/3 cup chopped walnuts

Preheat oven to 350 degrees. Using solid vegetable shortening, thoroughly grease a 9" x 5" x 3" loaf pan; set aside. In sifter, place flour, baking powder, baking soda and salt. Sift over a piece of waxed paper; set aside. In large bowl of electric mixer, at high speed, beat butter, sugar, egg and 1 teaspoon vanilla extract until smooth and fluffy. Continue to beat the mixture until ingredients are thoroughly combined. Set aside. Peel bananas; place in a medium-sized bowl and mash with a potato masher or fork (to yield 1 1/2 cups) until all large lumps are broken up. Add to the sugar-and-egg mixture and stir with a wooden spoon until well mixed. Add flour mixture, bran cereal and nuts, beating just until smooth. Turn banana-bran batter into the prepared loaf pan, spreading until smooth. Place pan on center rack in oven and bake for 60 minutes or until a cake tester inserted into center of bread comes out clean. Place pan on wire rack and let cool for about 10 minutes. Remove bread from pan and let stand on rack until it is completely cool.

Poppy Seed Bread
Yield: 2 loaves

Bread Ingredients:
3 cups flour
1 1/2 teaspoons salt
1 1/2 teaspoons baking powder
2 1/2 cups sugar
1 1/2 tablespoons poppy seeds
1 1/2 cups milk
3 eggs
1 1/2 teaspoon vanilla
1 1/2 teaspoon almond extract
1 1/8 cup cooking oil

Glaze Ingredients:
3/4 cup sugar
1/4 cup diluted orange juice
1/2 teaspoon vanilla
2 teaspoons margarine
1/2 teaspoon almond extract

Bread:
Mix all the liquid ingredients, then fold in the dry ingredients. Place batter into greased loaf pans. Bake at 350 degrees for 50-60 minutes.

Glaze:
Start this five minutes before the bread is done. Mix and bring the ingredients to a boil until all the sugar is dissolved. When the bread is done, loosen the sides of the bread from the pans, then pour the glaze over the bread. Let stand for 15 minutes. Remove from pan and cool.

Carrot Pecan Muffins
Yield: 12 large muffins

2 cups all purpose flour
1 tablespoon baking powder
2 teaspoons pumpkin pie spice
1/2 teaspoon salt
3/4 cup grated carrot (or summer squash or zucchini)
1/3 cup firmly packed light brown sugar
1 egg
3/4 cup milk
1/4 cup vegetable oil
1/2 cup chopped pecans
Strawberry Jelly

Sift flour, baking powder, pumpkin pie spice and salt into a medium bowl; stir in carrot and brown sugar until well blended. Beat egg in 2-cup glass measure with a fork; add milk and oil; pour over dry ingredients and stir just to blend; stir in pecans. Grease 12 large muffin pan cups or use paper muffin liners. Spoon in batter, dividing evenly. Make a thumbprint in the center of each muffin and spoon jelly into center. Bake at 400 degrees for 20 minutes or until golden brown. Cool in pan on wire rack 5 minutes; serve immediately.

Very Lemon Bread
Yield: 1 loaf

1/3 cup butter, melted
1 cup sugar
3 tablespoons lemon extract
2 eggs, lightly beaten
1 1/2 cups flour
1 teaspoon baking powder
1 teaspoon salt
1/2 cup milk
2 tablespoons freshly grated lemon peel
1/2 cup chopped pecans (optional)

Lemon Glaze:
1/4 cup fresh lemon juice
1/2 cup sugar

Mix butter, sugar, lemon extract and eggs. In separate bowl, sift flour with baking powder and salt. To butter mixture, add flour mixture alternately with milk, stirring just enough to blend. Fold in lemon peel and pecans. Pour batter into greased and floured 9" x 5" loaf pan and bake at 350 degrees for 1 hour or until wooden pick inserted in center comes out clean. Leave bread in pan and prick lots of holes in the top. While bread is still warm, drizzle lemon glaze mixture over top and sides. Wrap in foil and store for 1 day before slicing to serve. Can be frozen and sliced while still partially frozen.

Carrot Bran Muffins
Yield: 18 muffins

1 1/2 cup bran - unprocessed
1 1/2 cup whole wheat flour
1 teaspoon salt
1/2 teaspoon nutmeg
1 teaspoon cinnamon
1 1/2 teaspoon baking soda
2 tablespoons vinegar
1 1/2 cup milk (skim is OK)
1/3 cup honey
1 cup grated carrot
1/4 cup vegetable oil
1/4 cup molasses
1/2 cup raisins
1/2 cup nuts
2 eggs

Mix dry ingredients in large bowl. Mix all remaining ingredients in another bowl. Combine and mix just until dry ingredients are moistened. DO NOT OVER BEAT. Fill greased muffin tins or use muffin paper liners. Bake, at 400 degrees, for 20 minutes.

Carrot-Macadamia Muffins
Yield: 32 muffins

2 cups milk
2 teaspoons cider vinegar
1 cup water
1 1/2 cups shreds-of-wheat bran cereal
1 cup light brown sugar
1/4 cup molasses
1/2 cup vegetable oil
3 large eggs, at room temperature
2 1/4 cups unsifted all purpose flour
3 1/2 teaspoons baking soda
1 teaspoon salt
1 1/2 cup wheat bran flakes cereal
1 1/2 cups shredded carrots
7 oz. package chopped dates
3 1/2 oz. jar macadamia nuts, chopped

Mix milk with cider vinegar and let stand 30 minutes or until milk mixture is soured. After 20 minutes have passed, in a small saucepan, bring water to boiling and add to shreds-of-wheat cereal. Let stand for 10 minutes. In a large bowl of an electric mixer, at medium speed, mix brown sugar, molasses and vegetable oil until blended. Beat in eggs one at a time. Stir in milk mixture and the soaked shreds-of-wheat bran cereal. Mix together flour, baking soda and salt. Add flour mixture to the brown sugar mixture in bowl and beat at medium speed until blended. Stir in wheat bran flakes cereal, shredded carrots, chopped dates and chopped nuts. Cover and let batter stand for 1 hour at room temperature or up to 1 day in the refrigerator before baking. Preheat over to 400 degrees. Grease or line muffin tins with paper liners. Using an ice-cream scoop, spoon or measuring cup, divide batter evenly into prepared muffin tins filling each cup about two-thirds full. Bake for 25 minutes or until wooden pick inserted into center of muffin comes out clean.

Aileen's Bran Muffins

Yield: 50-60 muffins

4 eggs, beaten
3 cups sugar
1 cup oil
5 1/2 cups all purpose flour sifted with
5 1/2 teaspoons of baking soda
1 quart buttermilk
15 oz. raisin bran cereal
1 cup chopped nuts (optional)

In large bowl mix eggs and sugar. Add oil and mix well. Add flour by mixing 1 cup at a time - alternating with buttermilk. Mix in raisin bran cereal and nuts. Prepare muffin tins. Fill each muffin cup 2/3 full. Bake, at 375 degrees, for 12-15 minutes. Batter will keep in refrigerator for 3-4 weeks.

Sweet Potato Orange Muffins

Yield: 18-24 muffins

1 cup all purpose flour
1 cup whole wheat flour
2 teaspoons baking powder
2 teaspoons baking soda
1 teaspoon cinnamon
1/2 teaspoon nutmeg
1/2 teaspoon allspice
16 oz. can sweet potatoes, drained
2/3 cup brown sugar, firmly packed
2 eggs or 4 egg whites
1 cup orange juice
1 carrot, shredded
1 teaspoon vanilla
1 cup raisins (optional)

Preheat oven to 400 degrees. In medium bowl, combine flours, baking powder, soda, cinnamon, nutmeg and allspice. In a large bowl, mash sweet potatoes. Add sugar, eggs, orange juice, carrots and vanilla to mashed sweet potatoes. Add dry ingredients to liquid ingredients and mix well. Fill muffin cups until 3/4 full. Bake 15-20 minutes, until tops are brown. Let cool and remove from cups.

Make Ahead Buttermilk Scones
Serves 6

2 cups buttermilk, warmed
1 package dry yeast
1/4 cup warm water
1 tablespoon sugar
1 egg
1 tablespoon salad oil
3/4 teaspoon salt
1/2 teaspoon baking powder
1/4 teaspoon baking soda
4 cups flour

Soften yeast in 1/4 cup warm water. Combine warm buttermilk, sugar, egg, oil, salt, baking powder, baking soda, softened yeast and 2 cups flour. Beat until smooth. Add remaining flour to make moderately stiff dough. Cover and place in a warm place and allow to rise until double. Punch down. Cover and refrigerate overnight. Roll out 1/2" thick. Cut into pieces (approximately 4" x 3"). Fry in hot oil until golden brown, turning once. Will puff up as they cook. Serve with honey butter.

Honey Butter:
1 cup butter, softened
1/4 cup honey
1 egg yolk

Beat for 10 minutes. Keep refrigerated until needed.

Blueberry Banana Scones
Serves 6

1 1/4 cups all purpose flour
1/2 cup whole wheat flour
1/4 cup sugar
1 teaspoon baking powder
1/2 teaspoon baking soda
1/4 cup butter, cut into chunks
1/2 cup lemon flavored yogurt
1/3 cup mashed bananas
1/2 cup blueberries
1/4 cup finely chopped walnuts (optional)
1 tablespoon brown sugar (optional)

Preheat oven to 350 degrees. In a bowl combine flour, whole wheat flour, 1/4 cup sugar, baking powder and baking soda. Cut in butter until mixture resembles fine crumbs. Add yogurt, bananas, blueberries and nuts. Stir until moistened. Mound dough onto a lightly oiled baking sheet. With lightly floured hands, pat mound into a smooth 7-inch round. With a floured knife, cut halfway through the mound to make 6 wedges. Sprinkle top with brown sugar. Bake until golden brown, about 25 minutes. Cool on a rack and cut into 6 wedges. Serve warm.

Grocery Store

All of Park City's stores operated on credit until payday. Paydays were not scheduled and often a month elapsed between pay periods. The biggest challenge was to keep miners away from their ethnic clubs (saloons) before the bills were paid. When store bills were paid there was a sack of candy thrown in for the kids and if the miner was a regular customer, or one with a large bill, a jug of whiskey would be included "on the side."

Green Beans with Nuts and Lemon
Serves 8

1 1/2 lb. green beans, trimmed
1 to 2 tablespoons olive oil
2 teaspoons freshly grated lemon zest
1/2 cup hazelnuts, toasted until golden and chopped fine

In a kettle of boiling salted water, cook beans until just tender (3 to 8 minutes). Drain beans and toss in large bowl, while still hot, with the remaining ingredients.

Brussels Sprouts with Cashews
Serves 6-8

2 lb. fresh Brussels sprouts
3 cups water
3 chicken flavored bouillon cubes
1/3 cup butter or margarine
3/4 cup dry roasted cashew halves
1/4 teaspoon dried thyme
1/4 teaspoon salt
1/8 teaspoon pepper

Wash Brussels sprouts thoroughly. Combine water and bouillon cubes in medium saucepan. Bring to a boil. Add Brussels sprouts, return to boil. Reduce heat, cover, and simmer for 15 minutes or until tender. Drain well and place in serving bowl. Melt butter in small skillet. Add cashews and seasonings. Cook on low for 5 minutes. Pour over sprouts to serve.

Guess Again Carrots
Serves 8

2 lb. carrots, peeled and sliced
2 tablespoons butter or margarine
1 medium onion, grated
6-8 oz. sharp Cheddar cheese, grated
1/2 teaspoon salt
pepper, to taste
1/2 cup bread crumbs
parsley (garnish)

Boil carrots in a small amount of water until tender. Drain and mash. Add butter, onion, cheese, salt and pepper. Place in buttered casserole. Top with bread crumbs. Bake, at 350 degrees, for 40 minutes. Garnish with parsley.

Fall Casserole
Serves 6

3 1/2 lb. butternut squash
1 large red bell pepper, cut into
1 inch pieces
3 tablespoons olive oil
2 large garlic cloves, minced
3 tablespoons minced fresh
parsley leaves
1 1/2 teaspoons minced fresh rosemary
freshly ground pepper to taste
2/3 cup freshly grated Parmesan cheese

Preheat oven to 400 degrees. With a sharp knife cut squash crosswise into 2-inch thick slices. Working with one slice at a time, cut side down, cut away peel and seeds and cut squash into 1-inch cubes. In a large bowl, stir together squash, bell peppers, oil, garlic, herbs, black pepper and salt to taste. Transfer mixture to a 2-quart casserole dish and sprinkle evenly with Parmesan. Bake casserole in middle of oven until squash is tender and top is golden (about 1 hour).

Roasted Vegetables
Serves 4

1 yellow pepper, quartered, seeds and
ribs removed
1 red pepper, quartered, seeds
and ribs removed
1 bulb fennel, quartered
2 small winter squash, peeled,
quartered and sliced
2 small red onions, quartered
6 whole baby turnips
salt and pepper to taste
3 tablespoons extra virgin olive oil
1/4 cup balsamic vinegar
3/4 cup fresh thyme, chopped

In a bowl, mix together oil, vinegar, salt and pepper. Add vegetables and toss to coat. Place in casserole dish. Bake, at 350 degrees, for 30 minutes or until vegetables are soft. Remove from oven. Sprinkle with fresh thyme and serve.

French Green Beans
Serves 8-12

2 lb. frozen French cut green beans
1 medium onion, sliced
1 green pepper, cut in strips
4 oz. can whole mushrooms, drained
2 medium tomatoes
1/2 cup butter
2 teaspoons horseradish sauce
3 tablespoons brown sugar
1 teaspoon salt
pepper to taste

Put vegetables, except tomatoes, in 9" x 13" baking dish. Mix butter, horseradish mustard, brown sugar, salt and pepper and dot on top of vegetables. Bake, covered, at 400 degrees for 20 minutes. Add tomatoes the last 5 minutes.

Broccoli and Garlic
Serves 6

5 slices bacon
2 cloves garlic, cut into thin slivers
1/2 cup olive oil
1 1/2 lb. broccoli, flowerettes
and pieces
1/2 cup water
1/2 cup raisins
1/2 teaspoon salt
1/2 teaspoon crushed red pepper flakes
3 medium sized ripe tomatoes, diced
1/3 cup sliced almonds

Cook bacon until golden brown in skillet. Transfer bacon to paper towels. Drain all but one tablespoon of fat from the skillet. Add garlic slivers and olive oil. Sauté until golden brown. Remove garlic and discard. Add broccoli, water, raisins, salt and red pepper flakes to skillet. Cover the skillet and cook broccoli mixture for 5 minutes. Add tomatoes, reserved bacon and sliced almonds. Toss gently and heat only until tomatoes are warm. Serve immediately.

Cranberry Relish Mold
Serves 12

12 oz. package whole cranberries, picked over and rinsed
1 cup sugar
1 cup water
1 1/2 envelopes unflavored gelatin (about 4 1/2 teaspoons)
1/3 cup firmly packed light brown sugar
6 oz. can unsweetened pineapple juice
2 tablespoons red wine vinegar
2 cups coarsely chopped cooking apples
1 tablespoon prepared horseradish

Cook cranberries, sugar and 1/4 cup water in medium-size saucepan over medium-high heat, stirring occasionally, until cranberries pop and mixture starts to thicken (about 10 minutes). Set aside and cool completely. Sprinkle gelatin over 1/4 cup water in small saucepan. Let stand 5 minutes. Add remaining 1/2 cup water and brown sugar to gelatin. Cook over low heat, stirring occasionally, until gelatin and sugar are completely dissolved. Stir in pineapple juice and vinegar. Pour into large bowl and refrigerate until mixture is partially set, about 45 to 60 minutes. When thickened, fold in cranberry mixture, apples and horseradish. Pour into 6 non-aluminum decorative molds. Chill overnight until firm. Unmold onto serving platter.

Spiced Cranberry Sauce
Yield: 3-4 pints

2 lb. cranberries
1 1/3 cup vinegar
2/3 cup water
4 cups sugar
4 teaspoons ground cinnamon
1 teaspoon ground cloves

Cook cranberries in syrup made by combining vinegar, water, sugar and spices. Bring to boil, simmer, uncovered about 30 minutes. Mash berries with potato masher if crushed berries are desired. Refrigerate, freeze or can extra amount.

English Walnut Broccoli
Serves 8-10

3 10 oz. packages frozen broccoli, thawed
1/2 cup butter
4 tablespoons flour
4 teaspoons instant chicken bouillon or 4 bouillon cubes crushed
2 cups milk

Topping:
2/3 cup water
6 tablespoons butter
8 oz. package Pepperidge Farm herb crumbs
2/3 cup coarsely chopped walnuts

Place broccoli in a buttered 9" x 13" casserole pan. Make cream sauce by melting 1/2 cup butter and stirring in flour and bouillon. Add milk, cooking to a smooth sauce consistency. Pour cream sauce over broccoli. To make topping, melt butter in small pan with water. Pour over the stuffing mix in a bowl and toss. Add chopped walnuts. Spread over broccoli and cream sauce. Bake, at 350 degrees, for 30 minutes.

"The Best Ever" Grilled Vegetables
Serves 6

2 zucchini
12 mushrooms
1 eggplant, peeled
fennel
1 bell pepper
1 red onions
12 cherry tomatoes
1/2 - 3/4 cup mayonnaise
2 teaspoons lemon zest
1 teaspoon marjoram
salt and pepper to taste

Prepare the grill. Slice the vegetable into 1/2" to 3/4" pieces. In a large bowl mix the mayonnaise with the lemon zest and marjoram. Place the vegetable pieces into the bowl with the mayonnaise mixture and thoroughly coat all pieces. Thread the vegetables on metal skewers, alternating them. Salt and pepper to taste. Cook the vegetables over medium heat, turning kewers frequently until heated through and beginning to char. Remove and serve immediately.

Sweet Potato Casserole
Serves 12

4 lb. sweet potatoes
boiling water
1 teaspoon salt
6 medium bananas
1/4 cup orange juice
1/2 cup firmly packed light brown sugar
3/4 teaspoon ground cinnamon
2 tablespoons butter or margarine

Cook potatoes in large saucepan with salt and boiling water. Bring to a boil and reduce heat. Simmer for 30 to 35 minutes or until potatoes are tender. Drain, peel and cut potatoes into 1/4 inch slices. Preheat oven to 375 degrees. Grease 2-quart casserole thoroughly with butter. Peel bananas. Discard skins and cut bananas into 1/4-inch thick slices. In medium bowl, mix bananas and orange juice. In small bowl, mix brown sugar with ground cinnamon. Set aside. In bottom of prepared casserole arrange one third of the potato slices. Top with half of the banana slices and sprinkle with one third of the sugar mixture. Dot with one-third of the butter. Repeat layering. Bake casserole 45 minutes or until bubbly.

Potatoes Nicoise
Serves 6

1 clove garlic, halved
3 medium-sized potatoes, peeled,
cut into 1/4 inch slices
4 fresh tomatoes, peeled and
sliced into 1/2 inch slices
3 fresh parsley sprigs, chopped
1/2 teaspoon salt
1/4 teaspoon dried basil
1/4 teaspoon ground nutmeg
1/4 teaspoon dried tarragon
2 large red onions, thinly slices
2 tablespoons butter
1/2 cup shredded Gruyere cheese
or Cheddar cheese

Preheat oven to 400 degrees. Rub garlic in bottom of 1 1/2-quart shallow baking dish. Discard garlic. In small bowl combine parsley, salt, basil, nutmeg and tarragon. Place half of the potatoes in prepared casserole. Sprinkle with 1/2 parsley mix, 1/2 onions and 1/2 tomatoes. Repeat layers. Cut butter into small pieces and dot top of casserole. Cover casserole loosely with aluminum foil. Bake 45 minutes or until potatoes are fork-tender. Sprinkle top of casserole with cheese. Bake, uncovered, 5 minutes or until cheese is lightly browned.

Roasted Garlic Potatoes
Serves 4

4 large boiling potatoes, peeled
and cut into lengthwise pieces
4 cloves fresh garlic, minced
6 tablespoons butter
3/4 cup Parmesan cheese

Melt butter and add garlic. Cook on medium for 1 minute. Mix butter mixture, potatoes and 1/2 cheese until the potatoes are well coated. Pour into a shallow greased baking dish. Top with remaining cheese. Bake, at 400 degrees, for 30 minutes. Do not stir.

Garlic Mashed Potatoes
Serves 6

6 large russet potatoes
6 cloves garlic, peeled
1/4 cup milk
2 tablespoons butter
1/2 cup sour cream
2 oz. cream cheese
salt and pepper

Scrub potatoes and cube. Do not peel. Cover potatoes and garlic with water in saucepan and boil until tender. Heat milk and butter until butter melts. Drain potatoes and garlic. Beat in mixer until smooth. Add sour cream, cream cheese, salt and pepper, then milk mixture until potatoes are the consistency you desire. Can be made ahead and placed in covered casserole. If refrigerated, heat at 325 degrees for 45 minutes.

Au Gratin Potatoes
Serves 6-8

16 oz. package Velveeta Cheese, cubed
2 lb. frozen hash brown potatoes
1/2 cup butter or margarine
1 can cream of chicken soup
1 pint sour cream
2 tablespoons onions, minced

Combine all ingredients in 9" x 13" pan, mix well. Bake, at 350 degrees, for 1 hour 10 minutes, or until golden brown.

Baked Beans
Serves 6-8

6 slices bacon, fried crisp and diced
2 15 oz. cans red kidney beans,
drained
2 15 oz. cans green lima beans,
drained
28 oz. can regular baked beans
1 9.75 oz. jar chili sauce
1 cup onions, finely chopped
2/3 cup brown sugar
1/4 cup prepared mustard
1 tablespoon Worcestershire sauce
1 clove garlic, minced
1 teaspoon salt
1/2 teaspoon pepper

Combine all ingredients in crock pot. Simmer for 4 hours at high setting, stirring occasionally.

Bourbon Baked Beans
Serves 12

1 tablespoon dry mustard
2 tablespoons molasses
1/2 cup bourbon
1/2 cup "homemade" chili sauce
2 tablespoons instant coffee
1 cup brown sugar
4 tablespoons chopped onions
4 lb. "B & M" canned baked beans

Mix and cook first 8 ingredients in a saucepan until well blended, stirring often. Put canned baked beans in large casserole and mix in sauce. Bake uncovered, at 350 degrees, for 1 hour.

Chilies Rellenos
Serves 4

4 oz. Monterey Jack cheese, cut into strips
7 oz. can California green chilies, seeded and pith removed
4 eggs
1/3 cup milk
1/2 cup all purpose flour
1/2 teaspoon baking powder
1 cup shredded sharp cheddar cheese
Salsa (optional)

Prepare in morning or the night before. Divide the Monterey Jack cheese among chilies, folding or tucking cheese inside. Arrange chilies side by side in bottom of greased, shallow 1 1/2-quart baking dish. With an electric mixer, beat eggs until thick and foamy. Add milk, flour and baking powder. Beat until smooth. Pour batter over chilies, moistening evenly the surface of all chilies. Cover and refrigerate until ready to bake. Sprinkle with cheddar cheese. Bake, uncovered, at 375 degrees, for 30 minutes or until puffed and appears set when gently shaken. Serve with salsa, if desired.

Arroz con Chiles Verdes (Rice with Green Chilies)
Serves 6-8

3 cups sour cream
2   4 oz. cans chopped green chilies
3 cups cooked rice or shredded potatoes
salt and pepper to taste
3/4 lb. sliced Monterey Jack cheese
1/2 cup grated cheddar cheese

Thoroughly mix sour cream and green chilies. Season rice with salt and pepper to taste. Grease a 1 1/2-quart casserole dish. Layer rice, sour cream mix and monterey Jack cheese. Finish with rice on top. Bake, at 350 degrees, for 35 minutes. Add grated cheddar cheese for last 5 minutes.

Rice with Wine and Mushrooms
Serves 6

1 cup rice
4 tablespoons butter or margarine
1 cup chopped tomato
1 lb. mushrooms, sliced
1/2 cup chopped onion
3 cups chicken broth
1/2 cup red wine
salt and pepper to taste
1 cup thawed green peas
1/4 cup grated Parmesan cheese
(optional)

In large skillet, cook rice, tomato, mushrooms and onion in butter for 10 minutes, stirring frequently. Add broth, wine and seasonings. Mix well. Cover. Simmer for 25 minutes or until rice is tender and liquid is absorbed. Stir in peas and heat. Sprinkle with cheese.

Grilled Polenta with Tomato Herb Sauce
Serves 6

Polenta:
1 cup polenta
4 cups vegetable stock
1/2 cup butter
salt, pepper, Cajun spice,
Tabasco to taste

Polenta: Bring stock, butter and spices to boil. Slowly add polenta while stirring. Gently simmer 40-45 minutes. Pour into greased 12" x 12" baking pan and let cool. Then refrigerate covered for 1 hour. Oil and grill before serving with sauce.

Tomato Herb Sauce:
1 cup small diced Roma tomatoes
1/4 cup diced red onion
1 tablespoon chopped herbs (rosemary, thyme, basil, dill, parsley)
2 tablespoons balsamic vinegar
3/4 cup vegetable stock
2 tablespoons softened butter

Sauce: Heat a little oil and add onions and sauté until translucent. Add garlic for 30 seconds. Do not brown. Add tomato and sauté for 1 more minute. Add stock, vinegar and herbs. Reduce to 1/4 liquid. Add butter and stir until melted. Pour over grilled polenta.

Nora's Nutted Wild Rice
Serves 8-10

1 cup wild rice
5 1/2 cups chicken stock
1 cup pecan halves
1 cup yellow raisins
grated rind of 1 large orange
1/4 cup margarine
1/3 cup orange juice
1 teaspoon salt
pepper to taste

Cook wild rice in chicken stock. Drain. Mix rice and the remaining ingredients. Let mixture stand 2 hours to allow flavors to develop. Reheat and serve.

Tomato Dish
Serves 8

4 large tomatoes, sliced
2 medium onions, eighths
6 oz. pesto sauce
2 tablespoons olive oil
2 tablespoon pine nuts
2 tablespoons Parmesan cheese
4 cloves garlic, pressed

Slice tomatoes. Put 1/8 onions in a 9" x 13" pan. Put a dollop of pesto on each tomato. Sprinkle with pine nuts, Parmesan cheese and garlic. Sprinkle with olive oil. Bake, at 325 degrees, for 1 hour. Broil for 5 to 10 minutes.

Elaine's Fresh Cucumber Pickles
Serves 3-4

Dressing:
2 tablespoons sugar
1 teaspoon salt
1 teaspoon celery salt
1 tablespoon lemon juice
1/8 teaspoon freshly ground pepper
1/4 cup cider vinegar
1 long, narrow cucumber
1/4 cup chopped onion
2 tablespoons chopped parsley

Mix together dressing ingredients. Set aside. Draw the tines of a fork from one end of the cucumber to the other. Slice the cucumber in 1/8" or less slices. Do not peel. Add the cucumber slices, onion and parsley to the dressing. Refrigerate overnight before serving. Keeps well in refrigerator in a covered jar.

ENTREES

Silver King Consolidated Mine

The King Con Mine is one of the "entrees" in the history of Park City mines, but little remains of it today. The Claimjumper ski run passes directly over the site of the old mine. Famous names like Daly-Judge, Daly-West, Ontario, Silver King Coalition, American Flag, Crescent and Park City Con can be included in the list of Park City's most famous mines. During its long mining history, Park City produced more than 23 millionaires and over $500,000,000 in mining revenue. In 1929, stock market prices plummeted from $12.87 per share to $6.50 per share. There is still plenty of silver left in Park City, but the price per share of silver makes mining its ore no longer cost effective.

Italian Chicken and Pasta
Serves 4-6

2 tablespoons olive oil
1 lb. boneless, skinless chicken breasts,
cut into strips
1/2 teaspoon salt
1/4 teaspoon cracked pepper
1 small onion, cut into eighths
1 teaspoon minced garlic
6 oz. jar marinated artichoke hearts,
undrained, coarsely chopped
7 oz. jar roasted red sweet peppers,
undrained, coarsely chopped
1/2 cup pitted black olives, chopped
1/2 lb. tri-color fusilli
1/2 cup freshly grated Parmesan

Heat oil in heavy skillet over medium heat. Sprinkle chicken with salt and pepper. Cook chicken, onion and garlic over medium heat until chicken is cooked through (about 6 minutes), stirring occasionally. Drain. Stir in artichoke hearts, peppers and olives. Cook over medium-low heat until heated through (about 6 minutes). Meanwhile, cook pasta according to package directions until almost tender; drain. Transfer pasta to heated serving platter. Toss in Parmesan cheese and chicken mixture. Serve immediately.

Orange Tarragon Chicken
Serves 4-6

3 whole chicken breasts, halved,
boned and skinned
salt and freshly grated nutmeg, to taste
2 tablespoons butter
1 tablespoon orange marmalade
1/4 teaspoon tarragon
1 green onion, thinly sliced
1/3 cup white wine
1/4 cup whipping cream

Sprinkle chicken breasts with salt and nutmeg. In a large frying pan, heat butter over medium heat and brown chicken lightly. Add marmalade, tarragon, green onion and wine. Cover, reduce heat and simmer 10 minutes or until chicken is cooked through. Using slotted spoon, remove chicken breasts to heated dish. Add cream to liquid in pan. Bring to a boil, and stir, until sauce is reduced and slightly thickened. Salt to taste. Pour sauce over chicken.

Southwestern Oven-Fried Chicken
Serves: 4-6

3-4 lb. chicken pieces
3 slices white bread, torn in small pieces
(or 3/4 cup bread crumbs)
3 tablespoons fresh cilantro leaves
2 tablespoons yellow cornmeal
2 tablespoons pine nuts
(pecans or walnuts will do)
2 large cloves garlic, peeled
1 1/2 teaspoon ground cumin
1/2 teaspoon oregano leaves
1/2 teaspoon salt
1/4 teaspoon cayenne pepper
1/8 teaspoon ground cloves
1 egg white
2 tablespoons Dijon mustard
1 tablespoon water
2 teaspoons honey
1/4 teaspoon pepper

In food processor place bread crumbs, cilantro, cornmeal, pine nuts, garlic, cumin, oregano, salt, cayenne pepper and ground cloves. Process to form fine crumbs. Place mixture on a large shallow plate; set aside. In small bowl, mix together egg white, mustard, water, honey and pepper. Brush chicken pieces with egg mixture and gently press into bread crumbs to adhere the coating to the chicken pieces. Place chicken on rack in greased jelly-roll pan. Bake, at 400 degrees, about 40 minutes or until chicken is crisp and brown and fork can be inserted with ease.

Marinated Grilled Chicken Breasts
Serves 4-6

Marinade:
1 1/2 cup soy sauce
1/2 cup olive oil
2 Serrano chili peppers, halved, seeded and diced
1/3 cup honey
1/4 cup lemon juice
1 teaspoon minced garlic
3 tablespoons fresh thyme
(or 1 tablespoon dried thyme)
4-6 chicken breasts

Combine marinade ingredients in a bowl and set aside. Rinse chicken breasts and place between plastic wrap. Lightly pound until chicken is 1/4-inch thick. Place chicken breasts in marinade and refrigerate for 2 hours. Prepare the grill. Place the chicken on the grill and cook until done.

Chicken and Sausage Jambalaya
Serves 8

Seasoning mix:
2 whole bay leaves
1 teaspoon ground cayenne pepper
1 1/2 teaspoon salt
3/4 teaspoon white pepper
1 teaspoon thyme leaves
1/4 teaspoon black pepper
1/4 teaspoon sage

2 tablespoons unsalted butter
3/4 lb. smoked sausage
3/4 lb. boneless chicken, cut into bite-sized pieces (about 2 cups)
1 cup chopped onions
1 cup chopped celery
1 cup chopped green peppers
1 tablespoon minced garlic
1/2 cup canned tomato sauce
15 oz. can diced tomatoes
2 1/2 cup chicken broth
1 1/2 cups uncooked converted rice

Melt butter in large pot. Add sausage and cook until meat starts to brown, stirring frequently. Add the chicken and continue cooking until the chicken is cooked through. Stir in seasoning mix and 1/2 cup each of onions, celery, green peppers and garlic. Cook until vegetables start to get tender. Stir in tomato sauce and cook about 1 minute. Stir in remaining vegetables and can of diced tomatoes. Remove from heat. Stir in broth and rice, mixing well. Transfer into a 9" x 13" baking pan. Bake uncovered, in a 350 degree oven, until rice is tender, about 1 hour. Stir well and remove bay leaves before serving.

Apricot Chicken
Serves 6-8

8 chicken breasts, skinned and boned
4 oz. apricot jam
1 small bottle Russian dressing
1 package dry onion soup mix

Mix jam, soup and dressing together. Pour over chicken and bake, at 325 degrees, for 1 hour. Serve with rice.

Chicken Vegetable Casserole
Serves 4

6 small zucchini or 1 1/2 lb.
broccoli pieces
1 small onion
3/4 lb. chicken pieces, cut small
1 can cream of chicken soup
1 cup sour cream
1 1/2 teaspoons basil
2 cups Cheddar cheese, grated
1 box stove top stuffing
4 tablespoons margarine

Slice zucchini and onion into small pieces. Put in pot and cover with water. Cook for five minutes. Drain. While vegetables are cooking, fry chicken pieces in skillet sprayed with a vegetable oil spray. Place cooked chicken in medium bowl and add cream of chicken soup, sour cream, basil and cheddar cheese. Mix well. Then add cooked vegetables. Mix again. Prepare stuffing mix according to package directions but don't cook. Place half of stuffing mixture in bottom of casserole dish. Top with vegetable mix and then place remaining stuffing mix on top. Bake, at 350 degrees, for 25 minutes.

Easy Baked Chicken Breasts
Serves 6-8

6-8 boneless chicken breasts
8 oz. sour cream
2 tablespoons fresh lemon juice
1 1/2 teaspoons Worcestershire sauce
1 1/2 teaspoon celery salt
teaspoon paprika
1/2 teaspoon salt
pepper to taste
bread crumbs
4 tablespoons butter, melted

Marinate chicken breasts in mixture of sour cream, lemon juice, Worcestershire sauce, celery salt, paprika, salt and pepper overnight. Take out of refrigerator at least one hour before baking. Place in aluminum lined baking pan. Sprinkle generously with prepared bread crumbs. Drizzle melted butter over the chicken. Bake, at 350 degrees, covered for 45 minutes. Bake at 375 degrees uncovered for an additional 15 minutes.

Chicken Mostaccioli
Serves 4

4 chicken breasts, deboned, skinned
Italian salad dressing
1 cup marinated artichoke hearts,
quartered
2 1/2 oz. can sliced black olives
garlic salt and pepper to taste
2 cups Alfredo sauce, homemade
or packaged
16 oz. Mostaccioli pasta, cooked

Sauté chicken in Italian salad dressing until cooked through. Cut into 1 inch pieces. Prepare Alfredo sauce. Add all ingredients to sauce. Simmer 15 minutes. Serve over pasta.

Yellowstone Chicken
Serves 10-12

10-12 pieces of chicken
1 cup creamy Dijon salad dressing
1/2 cup teriyaki sauce
2 cloves garlic, crushed
cayenne pepper, to taste

Wash chicken. Barbecue over hot grill for 20 minutes turning occasionally. Combine other ingredients in bowl and mix by hand vigorously. Brush mixture over chicken and barbecue 20 minutes more, turning more frequently.

Chicken Bul-go-gee
Serves 4

4-5 boneless, skinless half
chicken breasts
1 cup oriental style sesame oil
1/2 cup soy sauce
7-8 garlic cloves, crushed
1 cup coarsely chopped scallions

Cut chicken breast halves lengthwise into three or four strips. Mix all other ingredients together in a medium bowl and add the chicken to marinade. Let chicken marinate for at least 45 minutes or up to 5 hours. Cook over hot coals or on a gas grill. Place strips perpendicular to the grill and cook 2-3 minutes per side.

Chicken Marbella
Serves 5-6

6-8 boneless chicken breasts, skinned
1 clove garlic, minced
2 tablespoons dried oregano
salt and pepper to taste
1/2 cup olive oil
1/2 cup red wine vinegar
1/2 cup pitted green olives, chopped
1 cup pitted prunes, chopped
1/2 cup capers with juice
6 bay leaves
1 cup white wine
1 cup brown sugar
1/4 cup fresh coriander (fresh cilantro),
finely chopped

In large bowl, combine everything except white wine, brown sugar and coriander. Arrange chicken in shallow baking pan. Pour marinade over it evenly. Sprinkle chicken pieces with brown sugar and pour white wine around them. Marinate overnight, refrigerated. Bake, at 350 degrees, for 45 minutes; basting frequently with pan juices. With slotted spoon, transfer chicken, prunes, olives and capers to a serving platter. Moisten with a few spoonfuls of juices and sprinkle generously with coriander or cilantro. Pass remaining juices in a sauce bowl.

Curry Chicken
Serves 6-8

6-8 pieces chicken
1/4 cup flour
salt and pepper to taste
1/4 cup butter or margarine
1/4 cup oil
1/3 cup cilantro, chopped fine
1 cup diced onions
2-3 garlic cloves, minced
1 tablespoon curry (or to taste)
2 cups canned tomatoes, mashed
with hands

Put flour, salt and pepper in a plastic bag. Add chicken pieces and shake to coat. Brown in butter and oil. Remove chicken, drain and place in a casserole. To pan drippings add cilantro, onions, garlic, curry and simmer gently until golden brown. Add tomatoes and simmer until pan is deglazed. Pour onion/tomato mixture over chicken and bake covered, at 350 degrees, for 40 minutes. Serve with toppings of your choice.

Toppings: raisins, cashews or peanuts, chutney, chopped green onions, chopped cilantro

Grilled Sesame Chicken
Serves 4-6

Marinade:
1/2 cup olive oil
1/2 cup white wine
1/2 cup soy sauce
1-2 tablespoons freshly grated ginger
1 tablespoon dry mustard
1 teaspoon freshly ground black pepper
4 cloves garlic, crushed
1/2 cup chopped green onions
3 tablespoons sesame seeds
2 whole chickens, quartered
or about 6 chicken breasts

Combine marinade ingredients. Place chicken in large zip-lock bag and pour in marinade. Squeeze out air and seal. Marinate refrigerated for 4-8 hours. Grill over medium-hot coals for 15-20 minutes, basting frequently with balance of marinade.

Turkey Meat Loaf
Serves 6

2/3 lb. ground turkey breast
1/3 lb. ground turkey dark meat
1 yellow or red pepper, diced
1 medium onion, diced
1 egg white or egg substitute
1/3 cup bread crumbs
2-8 cloves garlic, crushed
1/8 teaspoon each: thyme, marjoram,
basil and parsley
black pepper to taste
1 1/2 tablespoons Worcestershire sauce
1/4 cup catsup

Mix all ingredients until blended. Bake one hour at 350 degrees. Pour off liquid. Cover top of the loaf with more catsup and bake 15 minutes more. Let stand 15 minutes before slicing.

Cream Cheese Chicken
Serves 4

4 skinless, boneless chicken breast halves
8 oz. light cream cheese
2 eggs
1 cup flour
2 cups crushed club crackers
2 teaspoons poultry seasoning
1 tablespoon rosemary leaves
3/4 cup margarine or butter

Put 1/4 cup margarine in baking dish and melt. Pound each chicken half until flat. Put an inch thick piece of cream cheese on each chicken half and then roll. Dip the rolled chicken piece in the flour, then egg, then crushed crackers. Put in the pan with the melted butter. Sprinkle the poultry seasoning and rosemary leaves over the chicken. Melt the remaining margarine and pour over the entire chicken. Bake, at 350 degrees, for 1 hour.

King Ranch Chicken
Serves 6-8

12 corn tortillas
3 cups cooked chicken, shredded
1 can Rotel tomatoes with diced chilies
1 can cream of mushroom soup
1 can cream of chicken soup
2 cups grated cheddar cheese

Rip up the tortillas and lay in the bottom of a greased 9" x 13" pan or casserole dish. Mix the remaining ingredients, except the cheddar cheese, in a bowl. Pour mixture over the tortilla shells. Then sprinkle the grated cheese on top. Cover. Bake, at 350 degrees, for 30 minutes.

Turkey with Brandied Fruit Stuffing
Serves 12

Stuffing:
11 oz. box dried mixed fruit, coarsely chopped
1 cup water
1/4 cup brandy or orange juice
1 large onion, coarsely chopped
1/4 cup butter or margarine
2 tablespoons grated orange rind
1/2 teaspoon salt
1/4 teaspoon pepper
9 slices day-old whole wheat bread, cut into 1/2" cubes (6 cups)

For stuffing: Combine fruit, water and 2 tablespoons of brandy in large saucepan. Bring to boiling. Reduce heat to low; simmer 5 to 10 minutes or until fruit is tender. Drain and reserve any remaining liquid, adding, if necessary enough chicken broth or orange juice to liquid to make 1/2 cup. Set fruit aside. Sauté onion in butter in large skillet for 5 minutes or until tender. Stir in drained fruit, reserved cooking liquid mixture from fruit and remaining 2 tablespoons brandy, orange rind, salt and pepper. Place bread cubes in large bowl and pour fruit mixture over them. Toss gently with a fork to moisten all ingredients.

Turkey:
12 lb. turkey
3/4 teaspoon salt
1/2 teaspoon pepper
2 cups water
2 carrots, peeled and cut into 1" pieces
2 stalks celery, chopped into 1" pieces
2 medium-sized onions, peeled and quartered
4 parsley sprigs

Turkey: Preheat oven to 400 degrees. Remove neck and giblets and reserve for a gravy, if desired. Rinse turkey well with cold water, inside and out. Pat dry with paper toweling. Sprinkle inside of body and neck cavities with salt and pepper. Spoon stuffing loosely into both cavities. Tie legs to tail with string and skewer neck skin to back. Place turkey on rack in toasting pan with tight-fitting cover (or loose tent of foil). Add water, carrots, celery, onion and parsley. Roast turkey in preheated 400 degree oven for 15 minutes. Reduce oven temperature to 325 degrees, cover and roast 2 1/2 hours. Uncover and roast 45 minutes longer or until meat thermometer reaches 180 degrees. Let stand 20 minutes before carving.

Chicken Parmigiana
Serves 6

3 whole chicken breast
(1 lb. each), skinless, halved
1/2 cup seasoned dry bread crumbs
2/3 cup grated Parmesan cheese
1 large egg
1/4 to 1/3 cup olive oil
16 oz. spaghetti sauce
1 clove garlic, crushed
1 teaspoon dried oregano leaves,
crushed
8 oz. mozzarella cheese, cut in 6 slices
3 1/2 cup hot cooked pasta, such
as ziti or penne
2 tablespoons minced parsley

Preheat oven to 350 degrees. Combine bread crumbs and 1/4 cup Parmesan cheese. Set aside. Beat egg in shallow bowl. Dip chicken piece into beaten egg then dip chicken in crumb mixture. In large skillet, heat 1/4 cup of the olive oil over medium-high heat. Add chicken pieces and sauté for 5 minutes on each side turning once until golden brown. In a small bowl combine spaghetti sauce, garlic and oregano, mix thoroughly. Pour into a 9" x 13" baking dish. Arrange chicken pieces bone side down over sauce mixture. Cover loosely with aluminum foil. Bake 40 minutes. Remove foil and cover each chicken piece with a slice of mozzarella cheese. Sprinkle with remaining Parmesan and bake an additional 10 minutes longer or until cheese is lightly browned and sauce is bubbly. To serve, toss hot cooked pasta with 1 tablespoon olive oil and the minced parsley. Transfer pasta to the center of a serving platter and arrange chicken around the pasta.

Basil and Tomato Pasta Sauce
Serves 4-6

1/4 cup chopped onion
1 clove garlic, minced
1/4 cup olive oil
28 oz. can tomatoes, chopped
6 fresh basil leaves, chopped
1 teaspoon salt
1/2 teaspoon pepper
Parmesan cheese (garnish)

Sauté onion and garlic in oil in medium skillet until tender. Add tomatoes, basil, salt and pepper and bring mixture to a boil. Reduce heat and simmer for 15 to 20 minutes stirring occasionally. Cook pasta using package directions. Toss with sauce to coat. Garnish with fresh Parmesan cheese.

Raspberry-Grilled Hens
Serves 8

Marinade:
1/4 cup raspberry vinegar or white wine vinegar
1/4 cup orange juice
1/4 cup vegetable oil
1/2 cup fresh raspberries
3 small cloves garlic
1 teaspoon salt
1/2 teaspoon black pepper

4 (lb. each) Cornish game hens, split in half lengthwise
1 cup fresh raspberries (garnish)
spring greens (optional garnish)

In food processor or an electric blender, process marinade ingredients for 1 minute or until ingredients are thoroughly combined. Set aside. Rinse hens under cold water, pat dry with paper towels. Place hens in a shallow glass baking dish or in two jumbo self-sealing plastic bags. Pour raspberry marinade over hens. Refrigerate for 8 hours or overnight, turning occasionally. Place hens, skin-side down, 6 to 8 inches over red hot coals. Grill hens for 10 minutes or until lightly browned. Place hens, skin-side up on grill rack away from coals or gas heat. Brush hens on all sides with reserved marinade. Cover grill and cook the hens 35 minutes more brushing with marinade and turning as necessary. If desired, serve hens with raspberry and spring greens garnish.

Spinach Lasagna
Serves 12

Lasagna noodles
1 lb. ricotta cheese
1 lb. mozzarella cheese, grated
grated Parmesan cheese, to taste

Spaghetti Sauce:
28 oz. can Progresso crushed tomatoes
14 1/2 oz. can peeled tomatoes
1 onion
2 cloves garlic
1 tablespoon fennel, slightly ground
1 tablespoon basil
1 tablespoon parsley
1 tablespoon olive oil
1 bunch spinach, washed and chopped

Prepare sauce: Sauté onion, garlic, fennel, basil and parsley in olive oil until onions are translucent. Add crushed tomatoes and peeled tomatoes (puree before using). Simmer for 45 minutes, stirring occasionally. When nearly done place spinach in pan with sauce, cover, and cook until spinach is wilted. Cook lasagna noodles until al dente. In a 9" x 13" pan layer noodles, spinach spaghetti sauce, ricotta cheese, mozzarella cheese and Parmesan cheese to no less than 3 layers; ending with a topping of mozzarella. Bake, at 375 degrees, for approximately 30 minutes or until cheese is bubbling and slightly toasted.

Poached Chicken with Orange Sauce

Serves 8

4 lb. roasting chicken
salt
1/2 teaspoon ground cinnamon
1/2 teaspoon turmeric
1/8 teaspoon ground cloves
dash of pepper
water
1 tablespoon vegetable oil
2 cloves garlic, crushed
2/3 cup chopped onion
3/4 cup orange juice
2 tablespoons seedless raisins
3 tablespoons whole
unblanched almonds
2 teaspoons capers
2 tablespoons cornstarch
2 tablespoons orange zest, julienne
3 tablespoons orange marmalade
1 cup shredded romaine lettuce
(optional)
navel orange wedges (optional)
red grapes (optional)

Remove and discard neck and giblets from chicken. Rinse under cold water; drain and pat dry with paper towels. Sprinkle inside of chicken cavities with 1 teaspoon salt. Tuck wings under body; tie legs together at ends with kitchen twine. In a small bowl, combine 1/4 teaspoon salt, the cinnamon, turmeric, cloves, pepper and 1 tablespoon water. Stir to blend thoroughly. Brush the spice mixture evenly over entire chicken. Set chicken aside. Heat vegetable oil in a 6-quart Dutch oven over medium-heat until very hot. Add garlic and onion. Sauté, stirring constantly with a wooden spoon, until lightly browned. Stir in orange juice, 1/4 cup water, raisins, almonds and capers. Place chicken breast side up in Dutch oven. Cover; bring to boiling over medium-high heat. Reduce heat and simmer for 1 hour and 15 minutes or until chicken is tender. Baste chicken occasionally during cooking time with broth. Remove chicken to serving platter and discard string. Skim off and discard fat from broth. Stir cornstarch into 1/4 cup water; stir into broth, adding orange zest and orange marmalade. Cook mixture, stirring constantly with a wooden spoon until mixture turns clear and is thickened. Spoon some orange marmalade sauce over chicken and garnish platter with romaine lettuce, orange wedges and bunches of red grapes. Pass remaining sauce.

Chili-Cheese Chicken in Black Bean Sauce
Serves 8

4 whole chicken breasts, halved
(about 4 lb.)
1 2/3 cups shredded Monterey
Jack cheese
1 cup fresh bread crumbs
(about 3 slices of bread)
4 oz. can chopped green chilies
1/3 cup slivered almonds
1 1/4 teaspoon chili powder
1/4 teaspoon salt
1/8 teaspoon ground black pepper

Black Bean Sauce:
2 tablespoons vegetable oil
2 cups sliced green, red and yellow
peppers (1-inch pieces)
2 cloves garlic, crushed
15 oz. can black beans, undrained
3 tablespoons minced cilantro
1/2 cup chicken broth
1 tablespoon cornstarch

3 cups hot cooked white rice
lime wedge (optional)
sprigs of cilantro (optional)

Preheat oven to 350 degrees. Using a sharp knife, make a deep pocket in each chicken piece cutting between the tenderloin and the top portion of the meat. In a medium bowl, combine cheese, bread crumbs, chilies, almonds and 1/2 teaspoon of the chili powder. Mix well. Spoon about 1/4 cup of this filling into each chicken breast pocket; secure with metal skewers or wooden picks. Place stuffed chicken breasts in a shallow roasting pan; sprinkle with salt and pepper and remaining 3/4 teaspoon chili powder. Place in oven and roast 30 minutes. If a crisp skin is desired, broil 5 inches from heat source for 3 minutes. While chicken roasts, prepare Black Bean Sauce. In a large skillet, heat oil over moderately high heat. Add sliced peppers and the garlic. Sauté 5 minutes, stirring frequently with a wooden spoon. Stir in black beans and minced cilantro. In a small measuring cup, combine chicken broth and cornstarch; stirring until no lumps remain. Add to bean mixture in skillet. Bring to boiling, stirring constantly with a wooden spoon. Simmer until sauce thickens. Remove skewers from chicken breasts. Arrange chicken on a bed of hot cooked rice. Spoon some of the Black Bean sauce over the chicken; pass the remaining sauce. If desired, garnish with lime wedges and fresh cilantro.

Turkey Pesto
Serves 8

Pesto:
1 cup fresh basil leaves or 1 cup fresh
parsley plus 4 teaspoons dried
basil leaves
1/2 cup fresh parsley
3 cloves garlic
1 teaspoon grated lemon zest
1/3 cup grated Parmesan cheese
1/4 cup olive oil
1 lb. pasta, such as fusilli

6 tablespoons butter or margarine
2 lb. turkey cutlets, cut in 1/2 inch strips
1 large onion, sliced
1/2 lb. medium mushrooms, quartered
1/2 red pepper, cored, seeded
and cut into strips
1/2 yellow pepper, cored, seeded
and cut into strips
2 tablespoons freshly squeezed
lemon juice
2/3 teaspoon ground pepper
3 tablespoons toasted pine nuts

Prepare pesto. In a food processor with a steel blade, puree basil, parsley, garlic and lemon zest. Add grated Parmesan cheese. Process until well blended. With processor running, add olive oil and set aside.

Prepare pasta. In a large saucepan, bring water and 1 tablespoon salt to boiling over high heat. Add pasta and stir with a large fork to separate strands. Cook pasta until it is al dente, about 10 minutes. While pasta cooks, prepare turkey sauté.

Turkey sauté. In a skillet or large wok melt 3 tablespoons butter. Add half of the turkey at a time, stirring constantly with a wooden spoon, until turkey is cooked and browned. Remove browned turkey strips from skillet and place in a bowl. In the same skillet, melt remaining 3 tablespoons butter. Add onion, mushrooms and pepper strips. Cook 4 minutes, stirring constantly with a wooden spoon, until vegetables are crisp-tender. Return turkey to skillet. Stir in reserved pesto, lemon juice, salt and pepper. Cook until mixture is very hot, about 1 minute. Stir in pine nuts. Drain pasta and top with Turkey Pesto.

Broiled Chicken with Fettucine
Serves 2

3/4 cup julienne strips seeded vine-
ripened tomato
1/4 cup thinly sliced sun-dried tomatoes
(packed in oil)
1/4 cup thinly sliced red onion
1/4 cup finely chopped seeded jalapeno
chilies (wear rubber gloves)
1/2 tablespoons drained
green peppercorns
1 1/2 teaspoon finely chopped garlic
1 1/4 tablespoon fresh lemon juice
1/2 teaspoon salt
1/2 teaspoon freshly ground pepper
1 whole skinless boneless
chicken breast, halved
1/4 cup olive oil
7 oz. fettuccine
1/2 cup heavy cream
3 tablespoons brandy
3 tablespoons chopped fresh basil leaves

Preheat broiler.
In a bowl stir together tomatoes, onion,
jalapenos, peppercorns, garlic, lemon juice,
salt and pepper.

Brush chicken breast half with oil and season with salt and pepper. Broil chicken
about 4 inches from heat for 4 minutes on
each side, or until just cooked through.
Reduce temperature to 200 degrees and keep
chicken warm in oven. In kettle of salted
boiling water cook fettuccine until al dente.
Drain fettuccine and keep warm. In large
skillet sauté tomato mixture in oil over
moderately high heat, stirring 1 to 2 minutes. Stir in cream and brandy and simmer
until thickened slightly. Add fettuccine and
basil and stir. Divide evenly between two
bowls. Serve immediately.

Southwestern Corn Casserole
Serves 4-6

3 cups cooked corkscrew pasta
(12 oz. bag)
1 cup shredded jalapeno jack
cheese, divided
1 can cream of chicken soup
1/2 cup light sour cream
1 teaspoon chili powder
1/8 teaspoon garlic powder
8 oz. can corn, drained
4 green onions, chopped
4-6 poached chicken breasts, cubed or
shredded (or leftover turkey)

In greased 8" x 12" baking dish, combine
pasta and 1/2 cup of cheese. In medium
bowl combine soup, sour cream, chili powder, garlic powder, corn, green onions and
chicken. Spread evenly over pasta mixture.
Bake at 350 degrees for 30 minutes. Top
with remaining cheese. Bake 5 minutes
more. Serve with garnishes of your choice.

Garnishes: chopped tomato, chopped pitted
olives, sliced avocado, sliced green onions

Seafood with Spicy Tomato Chutney
Serves 4

Spicy Tomato Chutney:
1 teaspoon olive oil
2 tablespoons chopped shallots
5 fresh, ripe plum tomatoes, coarsely chopped (about 2 cups)
3 oz. package sun-dried tomatoes, diced
2-3 teaspoons finely chopped jalapeno pepper, to taste
1 sprig fresh thyme
1 tablespoon lemon juice
1 tablespoon honey
freshly ground pepper

16 large shrimp, peeled and deveined
12 scallops
8 oz. piece salmon fillet, skin and bones removed
salt and pepper to taste
2 tablespoons olive oil
1 medium size fennel bulb, trimmed, cut into thin slices
1/2 cup shallots, finely chopped
2 cloves garlic, crushed
1 cup dry white wine
1 1/2 cups chicken broth
2 tablespoons chopped fresh herbs (tarragon, Italian flat leaf parsley, chives, thyme)
French Bread

Tomato Chutney Sauce: Heat oil over medium low heat, add shallots and cook 2 minutes, stirring occasionally until soft. Add fresh and sun dried tomatoes, jalapeno pepper, thyme sprig and cook covered for 15 minutes until sun dried tomatoes are soft. Stir in lemon juice, honey and pepper. Cook, uncovered, 2 minutes longer until mixture is somewhat reduced. Remove from heat and discard thyme sprig. Set aside.

Seafood: Sprinkle shrimp, scallops and salmon with salt and pepper. In a non stick pan heat oil over medium-high heat and cook the shrimp, scallops and salmon until lightly browned, for about 1 minute per side. Transfer seafood to a cookie sheet lined with paper towels. To the drippings in the pan add the fennel, shallots and garlic. Cook for 4 to 5 minutes, stirring occasionally until the fennel is tender but still crisp. Remove the vegetables to the cookie sheet along with the seafood. Wipe out the pan with paper towels and add the wine. Boil until reduced to 1/2 cup. Add the chicken broth, bring to a boil. Reduce heat to low and simmer about 1 minute. Return the seafood and vegetables to the pan and cook 2 to 3 minutes longer. Remove from the heat, add the herbs and stir. Spoon into bowls. Serve with Spicy Tomato Chutney and chunks of crusty French bread.

Pad Thai
Serves 4

1/2 lb. uncooked linguine
3/4 cup tomato juice
3 tablespoon soy sauce
1 tablespoon vinegar
2 teaspoons sugar
3/4 teaspoon cornstarch
3 tablespoons oil, divided
1/2 lb. boneless, skinless chicken
breasts, cut into thin strips
2 cloves garlic, minced
1/2 lb. bean sprouts, rinsed and drained
1/3 cup green onions and tops
(1 bunch), sliced
1/2 lb. cooked baby shrimp,
rinsed and drained
1 tablespoon minced cilantro
lime wedges

Cook linguine according to package directions; drain. Meanwhile, combine tomato juice, soy sauce, vinegar, sugar and cornstarch; set aside. Heat 1 tablespoon oil in hot wok or large skillet over high heat. Add chicken; stir-fry 1 minute. Remove from pan. Heat remaining oil in same pan. Add garlic, bean sprouts and green onions; stir-fry 1 minute. Return chicken along with shrimp, cilantro and tomato juice mixture to skillet. Cook, stirring until sauce boils and thickens. Serve sauce over linguine and garnish with lime wedges.

Roasted Cornish Hens
Serves 2

2 tablespoons unsalted butter
3 teaspoons chili powder
2/3 teaspoon fresh lemon juice
1/4 teaspoon cayenne
1/4 teaspoon salt
a pinch of sugar
2 (1 1/2 lb.) Cornish hens,
split lengthwise

Preheat oven to 450 degrees. In a small bowl stir together butter, chili powder, lemon juice, cayenne, salt and sugar. Rinse and pat hens dry and arrange, skin sides up, on rack of a broiler pan. Loosen skin near breastbones and rub about 1 teaspoon chili butter under skin of each breast. Rub remaining chili butter on skin and roast hens in middle of oven until juices run clear when fleshy part of a thigh is pierced (about 25 minutes).

Shrimp in Butter Sauce
Serves 6

1/2 gallon water
1 tablespoon caraway seeds
1 tablespoon whole black pepper
1 tablespoon pickling spice
1 teaspoon cayenne pepper
1 bay leaf
1 teaspoon dry mustard
4 teaspoons salt
celery seeds

5-6 lb. unshelled shrimp

Sauce:
juice of 2 lemons
1 tablespoon Worchestershire sauce
7-8 dashes tabasco
1 teaspoon salt
1/2 lb. butter
1 tablespoon tarragon vinegar

In a large pan, boil water and spices for 20 minutes. Add shrimp and simmer for 20 minutes more. While shrimp cooks, combine sauce ingredients. Heat gently over low heat. Have guests peel their shrimp and dip in the sauce. Serve with a cobb salad.

Maple Glazed Salmon
Serves 4

4 .6 oz. salmon fillets
2 tablespoons olive oil
1 tablespoon herbs or Mrs. Dash
1/8 cup teriyaki marinade
1/4 cup maple syrup
1/2 cup brown sugar

Brush salmon fillets with olive oil. Sprinkle with herbs. Drizzle with teriyaki, then maple syrup. Sprinkle with brown sugar. Refrigerate at least 1 hour. Prepare charcoal or gas grill. Place fillets on sheet of heavy aluminum foil, then lay on grill. Close the grill cover and cook on medium heat for 20 minutes, or until salmon flakes easily with a fork.

Shrimp Creole
Serves 6

4 tablespoons butter
1 large onion, chopped
1 large stalk celery, diced
1 large green bell pepper, diced
2 cloves garlic, minced
1/2 teaspoon dried thyme
1/2 teaspoon salt
1/4 teaspoon white pepper
1/4 teaspoon cayenne pepper
1/2 teaspoon freshly ground
black pepper
1 tablespoon flour
1/4 cup white wine
1 cup tomatoes, peeled and diced
1 cup chicken stock
2 bay leaves
hot pepper sauce, to taste (optional)
2 lb. shrimp, shelled and deveined
6 to 8 cups cooked rice

In large skillet, sauté onions, celery, bell pepper and garlic in butter over medium heat until lightly browned. In small bowl, mix thyme, salt, white pepper, cayenne pepper, black pepper and flour. Stir into onion mixture and cook 2 minutes. Stir in wine, tomatoes, stock, bay leaves and hot pepper sauce. Reduce heat and simmer 20 to 25 minutes. Remove bay leaves. Stir in shrimp and simmer until shrimp are bright pink (3 to 4 minutes). Serve over hot rice. (Sauce can be prepared ahead. Add shrimp and cook just before serving.)

Easy Cajun Shrimp
Serves 4

3/4 lb. shrimp (36 count), cleaned
and deveined
2 tablespoons butter
2 tablespoons vegetable oil
1 tablespoon barbecue sauce
1 tablespoon lemon juice
1/4 teaspoon basil
1/4 teaspoon paprika
1/4 teaspoon rosemary
1/4 teaspoon red chili pepper
1/2 bay leaf
clove garlic clove, crushed

Sauté shrimp in butter and oil for 3 to 4 minutes. Add the remaining ingredients. Simmer for 4 to 5 minutes. Remove from heat. Let stand for 5 minutes before serving.

Scallops Au Gratin with Mushrooms
Serves 4-6

1 lb. scallops, cut into bite-sized pieces
1 cup chicken broth
1 cup sliced mushrooms
1/2 cup white wine
1 small onion, chopped
4 tablespoons butter or margarine
1/4 teaspoon garlic, minced
1 tablespoon parsley, chopped
1/2 cup shredded Swiss cheese
1 tablespoon cornstarch
1/2 cup milk
1/2 teaspoon thyme
3 cups cooked vermicelli or other pasta

Bring chicken broth to a boil over medium heat in a frying pan. Add scallops, reduce heat, cover and simmer until they are opaque (about 3 minutes). Lift scallops from pan with a slotted spoon. Set aside. Pour broth into measuring cup (about 1 cup total). Melt 2 tablespoons butter, add mushrooms and wine and cook 2 minutes. Reserve mushrooms. Pour juices into reserved chicken stock. Melt 2 tablespoons butter and add onions and garlic. Cook until soft. Add cornstarch diluted in a small amount of milk. Cook until bubbly. Remove from heat. Stir in reserved chicken stock. Return to heat and cook until sauce thickens. Stir in mushrooms, milk and thyme. Remove from heat, stir in parsley, scallops and half of the cheese. Put 1/2 cup of vermicelli in scallop shells or 1 1/2 cup ramekins. Divide mixture evenly and sprinkle with remaining cheese. Bake uncovered, at 400 degrees, for 12 to 15 minutes or until hot.

Pesto Pasta
Serves 6

oil
1 onion, diced
2 red peppers, diced
1 box frozen corn
7 oz. can diced green chilies
1-2 diced jalapeno peppers
10 oz. prepared fresh pesto sauce
1 lb. fettucine, cooked

In large heavy skillet, cook onion and the peppers in small amount of oil to soften. Add frozen corn, diced green chilies and pesto sauce until hot. Add diced jalapenos sparingly, according to taste. Serve immediately over hot fettuccine.

Tortellini Romeo and Julieta
Serves 2

9-12 oz. fresh or frozen tortellini
1 tablespoon unsalted butter
1/2 lb. medium shrimp, shelled
and deveined
1 tablespoon Sharwood's Bengal
Hot Chutney
1 teaspoon curry powder
1 cup heavy whipping cream
1/4 cup grated Parmesan cheese
2 tablespoons pomegranate seeds
(optional)

Cook tortellini in a large pot of boiling water until the tortellini begins to float to the top (about 5 minutes). Drain and set aside. In a non-stick skillet or sauté pan, melt the butter over medium-high heat and sauté shrimp for 2 to 3 minutes, just until pink. Put the shrimp aside with the cooked tortellini. In the same skillet, briefly cook the chutney over medium heat, stirring about 30 seconds. Then add the curry powder and heavy cream to the skillet. Cook for a few minutes, stirring occasionally, until the cream begins to simmer. Add cooked tortellini and shrimp to the pan with the curry-cream-chutney sauce and heat through, about 1 minute. Garnish individual plates with pomegranate seeds sprinkled on top and serve with freshly grated Parmesan cheese.

Carolyn's Pasta
Serves 2-4

1 lb. pasta
8 tablespoons olive oil
4 cloves garlic, minced
1 tablespoon anchovy paste
2 teaspoons capers
1/4 teaspoon red pepper flakes
1/3 cup parsley, chopped
1/2 cup bread crumbs
Parmesan cheese

Cook pasta according to package directions. While pasta cooks, heat oil in saucepan. Cook garlic and anchovy paste for 3 minutes. Add capers, red pepper flakes and half of parsley. Stir on medium-low heat. Drain pasta. Add sauce, bread crumbs and remaining parsley to pasta. Toss. Garnish with Parmesan cheese. Serve immediately.

Grilled Salmon Steaks with Lemon-Dill Sauce
Serves 4

Lemon-Dill Sauce:
1 2/3 tablespoons butter or margarine
1 1/2 teaspoon cornstarch
1/2 cup cold water
1/3 cup freshly squeezed lemon juice
1 tablespoon snipped fresh dill
(or 1 teaspoon dried dill)
1/2 teaspoon salt
1/8 teaspoon dried chervil leaves
dash of cayenne pepper
3 thin slices lemon, unpeeled,
cut in quarters

4 center-cut salmon steaks,
about 1-inch thick
2 whole lemons
dill sprigs (optional garnish)

Prepare Lemon-Dill Sauce: In a small saucepan, melt butter over moderately high heat; remove from heat. Combine cornstarch with water; stir into butter in saucepan. Add lemon juice, dill, salt, chervil and cayenne pepper; stir to blend. Bring sauce to boiling over moderate heat, stirring constantly. Cook until sauce thickens and turns clear. Remove from heat and add lemon quarters. Cover and set aside. Salmon: Cut off ends of lemons and cut in half. Secure one-half lemon slice into the opening of each salmon steak and secure with wooden picks. Heat barbecue grill. Cook salmon steaks 6 to 8 inches above coals. Cook for 10 to 15 minutes, turning once. Garnish each salmon steak with fresh dill sprig and a spoonful of hot lemon-dill sauce over each steak. Serve remaining sauce separately.

Salmon Patties
Serves 4

16 oz. can red salmon, drained
and flaked
4 eggs, slightly beaten
salt and pepper to taste
1 cup sour cream
1 cup crushed cornflakes
2 tablespoons minced green onions
oil

Mix all ingredients (except oil) in bowl. Place mixture in refrigerator for 15 minutes. Shape into patties. In large skillet, heat oil and brown salmon patties on each side. Can be served warm or cold.

Cashew Fish Fillets
Serves 6

3 tablespoons butter or margarine
1 egg
1 cup Romano cheese
2 tablespoons all purpose flour
6 sole or turbot fillets (4 oz. each)
3 tablespoons vegetable oil
2/3 cup chopped unsalted dry-roasted
cashew nuts

Tartar Sauce:
1/2 cup mayonnaise
1 tablespoon freshly squeezed
lemon juice
1/2 teaspoon Worcestershire
2 tablespoons sweet pickle relish,
drained
1 1/2 tablespoons finely chopped
shallot or green onion
1 tablespoon tiny capers, drained
1/8 teaspoon salt
1/8 teaspoon freshly ground pepper

lemon wedges and parsley sprigs
(garnish)

Preheat oven to 425 degrees. Place 3 table-spoons butter in a 10" x 15" jelly-roll pan or large shallow rimmed baking pan lined with aluminum foil. Place pan on center rack of oven for 3 to 4 minutes until butter melts. Remove from oven and swirl vegetable oil with butter. Place egg in a pie plate and beat slightly with a wire whisk. On a piece of waxed paper, combine Romano cheese and flour; mix thoroughly. Dip fish in the beaten egg and roll in cheese mixture. Arrange coated fish in pan, turning once to coat with butter-oil mixture. Sprinkle fillets with chopped cashews. Bake on top rack of oven for 10 minutes or until fish flakes easily. In a small bowl combine all tartar sauce ingredients. Stir with wooden spoon until blended. Refrigerate until ready to use. Serve fish garnished with lemon wedge and parsley sprig.

Crab Royal
Serves 4

1 egg
1/3 cup mayonnaise
1/8 teaspoon dry mustard
2 teaspoons Worcestershire sauce
1 tablespoon freshly squeezed
lemon juice
2 cups fresh crab meat or 15 oz.
canned King crab meat
1 1/2 tablespoons capers, drained
3 tablespoons green pepper, seeded
and chopped
2 slices white bread, cubed
1/2 cup grated American
or Cheddar cheese
1 lemon, sliced (garnish)
parsley (garnish)

In a medium-sized bowl, place egg, mayonnaise, dry mustard, Worcestershire sauce and lemon juice. Use a wire whisk or a small wooden spoon to mix ingredients thoroughly. Add crab meat, capers and green pepper to the egg-mayonnaise mixture. Toss gently. Broil bread cubes, 4 to 6 inches from heat, for 30 to 60 seconds, turning as necessary. Add to crab mixture and toss gently. Preheat oven to 400 degrees. Divide crab mixture evenly into large scallop shells, ramekins or 1-quart ovenproof baking dish. Bake for 10 minutes. Sprinkle with grated cheese and bake 5 minutes more or until cheese is melted and bubbly. Garnish with lemon slices and parsley.

Cod Mediterranean
Serves 2

1/3 cup Kalamata black olives,
pitted and diced
1 plum tomato, seeded and chopped
1 shallot, minced
1 1/2 tablespoons julienne fresh
basil leaves
1 tablespoon drained capers
1/2 teaspoon freshly grated orange zest
1 teaspoon fresh lemon juice
2 tablespoons olive oil
freshly ground pepper
2 6 oz. pieces cod fillet

In a bowl stir together olives, tomato, shallots, basil, caper, zest, lemon juice and 1 tablespoon oil to make salsa. Season with freshly ground black pepper. Season cod with salt. In a non-stick skillet heat remaining tablespoon oil over moderately high heat until hot but not smoking and cook cod about 4 minutes on each side, or until golden and cooked through. Spoon sauce over cod and garnish with basil sprigs.

Fish Paella

Serves 4

2 1/2 cups water
1 bay leaf
2/3 teaspoon dried thyme leaves
3/4 lb. boneless cod, cut into
1-inch cubes
2/3 lb. medium shrimp, shelled
and deveined
8 mussels
2 tablespoons olive oil or vegetable oil
1 onion, chopped
1 1/4 cup uncooked long grain
white rice
1 clove garlic, minced
2 medium tomatoes, peeled and
cut in 8 wedges each
1 teaspoon salt
1/4 teaspoon saffron threads, crumbled
1/3 cup frozen peas
2 tablespoons chopped fresh parsley
lemon wedges

Preheat oven to 325 degrees. In a large saucepan, combine water with bay leaf and thyme. Bring to boiling over high heat; add cod, the shrimp and the mussels. Reduce heat to low and simmer 2 minutes. Using a slotted spoon, gently transfer seafood to a large bowl. Remove and discard bay leaf. Reserve liquid in saucepan for later use. In an ovenproof Dutch oven, paella pan or large ovenproof skillet, heat 2 tablespoons oil over moderately high heat. Add chopped onion and sauté 2 to 3 minutes, stirring frequently with a wooden spoon, until onion is soft and tender but not browned. Add uncooked rice and minced garlic to Dutch oven; sauté 3 minutes, stirring constantly with a wooden spoon until rice is coated. Stir tomato wedges into rice mixture and cook until tomatoes are broken up and liquid in skillet evaporates. Pour reserved liquid into pan. Add salt and saffron. Bring to boiling over high heat, reduce heat to low and simmer uncovered for 10 minutes. Add peas and reserved seafood. Transfer to oven and bake uncovered until rice is tender, about 20 minutes. Remove from oven; cover and let stand 10 minutes. Uncover and garnish with lemon wedges and parsley. Serve immediately.

Scallops Linguine
Serves 6

1 tablespoon olive oil
2 medium cloves garlic, crushed
2 shallots, minced
2 tablespoons minced fresh basil or 2
teaspoons dried basil leaves
2 tablespoons minced Italian parsley
salt and pepper to taste
1/8 teaspoon cayenne pepper
16 oz can whole tomatoes
1/2 cup dry white wine
3 tablespoon tomato paste
1 tablespoon vegetable oil
8 oz. whole wheat linguine or spaghetti
1 lb. sea scallops
9 oz. frozen artichoke hearts, thawed
3 tablespoons pine nuts
parsley (garnish)

In a 3-quart saucepan over medium heat, heat 1 tablespoon olive oil. When oil is hot, add garlic and shallots. Cook, stirring constantly with a wooden spoon, until garlic and shallots are tender but not brown. Remove from heat. Add basil, parsley, salt and peppers, tomatoes, wine and tomato paste to mixture in saucepan. Return to heat and bring mixture to a boil, stirring to break up large pieces of tomato. Cover, reduce heat and simmer 20 minutes. In a 4-quart saucepan, bring 3 quarts water, 2 teaspoons salt and 1 tablespoon vegetable oil to a rolling boil. Add linguine; stir to separate strands. Cover saucepan until water returns to boiling. Uncover and cook linguine 8 to 10 minutes or until tender. Drain. While linguine cooks, add scallops and artichoke hearts to tomato mixture. Cook 5 minutes or until scallops are tender. Set aside. Place pine nuts in a small skillet and stir constantly over moderate heat until pine nuts turn golden brown. Remove from heat and set aside. Place linguine on large serving platter. Spoon tomato mixture over pasta. Sprinkle with pine nuts. Garnish with parsley. Serve immediately.

Grilled Mozzarella Cheeseburgers with Tomato Pesto
Serves 6

Dried Tomato and Arugula Pesto:
1 1/2 cups packed arugula, washed
1/3 cup bottled dried tomatoes packed in oil, drained
1/4 cup olive oil
4 tablespoons freshly grated Parmesan
3 tablespoons pine nuts, toasted golden and cooled
1 large clove garlic, chopped and mashed to a paste with
1/2 teaspoon salt
a pinch of sugar

1 large red onion, thickly sliced
2 lb. ground beef
1 cup dried tomato pesto
6 oz. mozzarella, cut into 6 slices
olive oil for brushing onion
6 hamburger buns, grilled lightly, if desired

Prepare pesto: In a food processor blend together all the pesto ingredients until smooth. Set aside. Cut six 1/4" thick slices from center of onion and reserve. Divide beef into 6 portions. Form indentation in each portion and spoon rounded teaspoon pesto into each indentation. Form beef portions into six 3/4" thick patties, enclose pesto completely. Grill patties on an oiled rack about 5 to 6 inches over glowing coals. Grill 5 minutes and turn burgers. Grill 3 minutes more. Top burgers with mozzarella and grill 2 minutes more, or until just cooked through. Transfer burgers to platter and let stand while grilling onions. Brush onion with oil and grill until softened and browned, about 3 minutes per side. Spread pesto on both sides of buns and make sandwiches with onions and burgers.

Olga's Tomato Basil Pasta
Serves 3-4

1/4 cup fresh basil, chopped fine
1/2 cup olive oil
1 cup fresh tomatoes, diced
3 cloves garlic, minced
1 teaspoon salt
1/4 teaspoon pepper
1 lb. cooked angel hair pasta
1 cup grated Parmesan cheese

Marinate first four ingredients 24 hours or overnight. Cook pasta as directed. Thoroughly drain water. Add salt and pepper to tomato mixture. Toss with cook pasta. Serve immediately. Sprinkle with Parmesan cheese as desired.

Amish Sandwich
Serves 6

2 tablespoons yeast
1 tablespoon sugar
1/2 cup warm water
2 cups buttermilk
5 tablespoons butter
4 tablespoons sugar
1 teaspoon salt
1/2 teaspoon soda
1 teaspoon baking powder
2 eggs
5-6 cups flour

Filling:
1 lb. ground beef, cooked
1 can cream of chicken soup
3 scallions, chopped fine
salt and pepper to taste
1/2 teaspoon caraway seeds (optional)
1/2 cup sour cream

Dissolve yeast and sugar in warm water. Heat buttermilk, butter, sugar, salt, soda, baking powder and eggs until warm. Add to yeast mixture. Add flour. Knead and mold into rolls. Mix filling ingredients together. Fill each roll with meat mixture. Let rise 45 minutes. Bake, at 350 degrees, for 15 to 20 minutes until golden brown. Baste with butter.

Shredded Beef Burritos
Serves 16

5 lb. beef rump roast
1/2 lb. bacon, cooked and crumbled
3 potatoes, cubed
1 large onion
1 lb. grated cheddar cheese
flour tortillas
green chili salsa or regular salsa

Cook roast that has been seasoned heavily with seasoning salt. Shred beef. Cook and crumble bacon. Cook cubed potatoes and onions in bacon grease until tender but not too soft. Remove from heat, add shredded beef and grated cheese. Put mixture in center of flour tortilla. Fold ends up and roll tightly. Serve with cold green chili salsa or regular salsa.

The Best (Microwave) Meat Loaf
Serves 6-8

2 lb. ground beef
1 package onion soup mix
1 green pepper, chopped
2 cups shredded bread
2 to 3 eggs
1/2 cup catsup
3 tablespoon prepared mustard
1/4 cup brown sugar
salt and pepper to taste

Topping:
2 tablespoons catsup
1 tablespoon prepared mustard
1 tablespoon brown sugar

Mix first 9 ingredients together and put into a round microwaveable casserole and put a glass in the center (or use a microwave bundt pan). Mix topping ingredients together and spread over meat mixture. Bake on high in the microwave for 10 minutes. Turn and bake 10 minutes more.

Italian Beef
Serves 20

4-5 lb. beef rump roast
3 cloves garlic (2 sliced and 1 chopped)
2-4 tablespoons of fennel seeds
8 cups beef broth
1 cup green peppers, chopped
4 tablespoons Worcestershire
2 teaspoons each: marjoram, thyme, oregano
salt and pepper to taste
Tabasco to taste

Slice 2 cloves of garlic lengthwise. Cut slits into roast and push garlic into slits. Sprinkle roast with fennel seed. Put onto open rack in roasting pan. Add beef broth to roasting pan. Roast at 325 degrees for 20 minutes for each pound of meat. Do not over cook. Meat should be rare. Cool. Slice paper thin (have your local butcher slice meat for you for a paper thin slice). Add remaining ingredients to juice. Simmer 15 minutes with the sliced beef. Refrigerate overnight. Simmer on low again for 2 hours before serving. Serve on rolls.

Barbecued Beef Brisket
Serves 10-12

6-7 lb extra lean beef brisket
1 tablespoon salt
1 tablespoons onion salt
2 tablespoons celery seed
1 tablespoon liquid smoke
1 tablespoon coarse pepper
1 tablespoon garlic salt
2 tablespoons Worcestershire sauce

Barbecue Sauce:
1/4 cup honey
2 tablespoons Dijon mustard
1 tablespoon parsley
1/4 teaspoon liquid smoke
1/4 cup brown sugar
1 cup ketchup
1 tablespoon Worcestershire sauce
1/4 cup lemon juice
1/4 cup soy sauce
1/4 cup vegetable oil

Begin brisket preparations two days before serving. Mix salt, onion salt, celery seed, liquid smoke, pepper, garlic salt and Worcestershire sauce together. Rub mixture over meat and let set in refrigerator for 24 hours. Bake after the 24 hours at 250 degrees for 12 hours (great to do overnight). Cool, pour off liquid and scrape pepper mixture off meat. Combine barbecue sauce ingredients. Slice meat into 1/4 inch slices and cover with barbecue sauce. Heat, at 350 degrees, for 1 hour.

Barbecued Ribs
Serves 4

2 tablespoons apricot-pineapple preserves
1/2 cup ketchup
3 tablespoons brown sugar
1 cup barbecue sauce
1 teaspoon horseradish sauce
shake or two of Worcestershire sauce
2 slabs of baby back ribs

Mix together first 6 ingredients. Set aside. Brown ribs in very hot oven. Take out and cover with sauce. Cover with foil and bake, at 325 degrees, for 1 1/2 to 2 hours.

Oyster Steak
Serves 4

4 2" thick beef filet mignons
(or rib eye steaks)
4 oz. bleu cheese
pint of fresh oysters
salt and pepper to taste

Cut a pocket in the middle of the steak from end to end leaving only a small slit for an opening. Stuff the steak with a mixture of half oyster and half bleu cheese. Seal opening of steak with toothpicks. Cook stuffed steak over grill on indirect heat until desired doneness. Salt and pepper to taste.

Pork Cutlets with Raisins
Serves 4

1 egg
water
1/3 cup all-purpose flour
2 teaspoons salt
1 lb. pork tenderloin cutlets
4 tablespoons butter or margarine
12 oz. fresh spinach fettucine
3 tablespoons freshly grated
Parmesan cheese
1/2 cup dark seedless raisins
1 chicken-flavored bouillon cube
1 tablespoon brown sugar
1 teaspoon julienne lemon zest
1/2 cup dry vermouth
1 tablespoon freshly squeezed
lemon juice
1 tablespoon minced parsley
2 small acorn squash, sliced and
steamed until tender
parsley sprig, garnish

In a pie plate, beat egg with 1 tablespoon water until thoroughly mixed. On a sheet of waxed paper, mix together flour with 1/2 teaspoon salt. Dip one pork cutlet at a time into the egg mixture and then dip in flour. Melt 2 tablespoons butter in skillet and add pork cutlets. Sauté 2 minutes on each side. While cutlets cook, bring 3 quarts of water and remaining 1 1/2 teaspoons salt to a boil. Add fettuccine and cook 3 to 5 minutes or until al dente. Drain and toss with remaining butter and the Parmesan cheese. In the skillet used for cooking the cutlets, add 1/2 cup water, the raisins, bouillon cube, brown sugar, lemon zest, vermouth and lemon juice. Bring to a boil and stir constantly over low heat until liquid is reduced to 3/4 cup. Arrange cutlets on a serving dish. Top with sauce and sprinkle with minced parsley. Surround with fettuccine and steamed squash. Garnish with parsley.

Light Vegetable Lasagna
Serves 8

12 lasagna noodles
1 tablespoon olive oil
1 yellow squash, quartered lengthwise
and sliced
1 zucchini, quartered lengthwise
and sliced
1 large yellow pepper, cored, seeded
and sliced
1 large red pepper, cored, seeded
and sliced
1 lb. broccoli cut into flowerets
3 cloves garlic, chopped
4 teaspoons fresh chopped thyme or
1 1/2 teaspoon dried
1 teaspoon salt

Cheese mixture:
2 eggs
15 oz. part-skim milk ricotta cheese
16 oz. low-fat dry-cured cottage cheese
1/2 cup fresh basil leaves, chopped
1/4 teaspoon red pepper seasoning
2 cups shredded part skim-milk
mozzarella cheese
fresh thyme sprigs (garnish)

6 cups of your favorite tomato
spaghetti sauce

Prepare noodles. Coat 9" x 13" pan with non-stick spray. Heat oil in pan. Add squash, sweet peppers, broccoli, garlic, thyme. Cover and cook until crisp tender. Drain liquid. Sprinkle with salt. Prepare cheese mixture: beat eggs in large bowl until blended. Stir in ricotta and cottage cheese, basil and red pepper seasoning until blended. Line pan with three noodles. Spread 2 cups cheese mixture, 3 cups of tomato sauce and layer with 3 noodles. Spread 3 cups vegetables, sprinkle with 1 cup mozzarella cheese. Cover with 3 noodles. Spread with remaining tomato sauce and cheese mixture. Top with remaining noodles and vegetables. Sprinkle with remaining mozzarella cheese. Cover with foil. Bake, at 425 degrees, for 1 hour. Garnish with thyme.

Mexican Corn Pie
Serves 4-6

3 large eggs
1 cup cream style corn
10 oz. package frozen corn
1 1/2 green onions, chopped fine
1/2 cup yellow corn meal
1 cup sour cream
4 oz. Monterey Jack cheese, cut into
1/2" cubes
4 oz. sharp Cheddar cheese, cut into
1/2" cubes
4 oz. chopped mild green chilies
1/2 teaspoon salt
1/4 teaspoon Worcestershire sauce
1/2 cup red pepper, diced (optional)

Grease 10" pie plate generously with Pam. In a large bowl, beat eggs. Add remaining ingredients and stir until thoroughly mixed. Pour into pie plate and bake uncovered, at 375 degrees, for 1 hour. The pie may be baked and then kept in the refrigerator for up to 3 days. Reheat refrigerated pie at 350 degrees for about 20 minutes. (Also makes a great side dish with barbecued ribs or chicken.)

Cheese Fondue
Serves 6

1 clove garlic, minced
1/4 cup butter
1/4 cup flour
2 cups half & half
1/2 lb. Swiss cheese, grated
1/2 lb. Cheddar cheese, grated
1 lb. American Processed cheese, cubed
3/4 cup dry white wine, warmed
2 tablespoons brandy
salt and nutmeg, to taste

bread chunks or vegetables for dipping

In double boiler or heavy saucepan, make a cream sauce with garlic, butter, flour and cream. Add cheese and mix until smooth. Add warmed wine, brandy, salt and nutmeg. If mixture seems too thick, add more cream until smooth for dipping. Serve with chunks of bread or vegetables.

Vegetable Polenta Pie
Serves 6

1/2 onion, chopped
1/2 green pepper, chopped
2 ribs celery, diced
2 tablespoons cooking oil, divided
3 medium zucchini, chopped
1 cup vegetable stock or water
1/4 teaspoon chili powder
1/4 teaspoon ground cumin
1/4 teaspoon oregano
1 teaspoon salt
dash of pepper
1/4 cup chopped parsley
1/4 cup whole wheat flour
1/4 teaspoon baking soda
1/2 teaspoon baking powder
1/2 cup cornmeal
1 egg
1/2 cup buttermilk
1 teaspoon brown sugar
1/2 cup cheddar cheese, grated

Sauté onion, green pepper and celery in 1 tablespoon of oil until soft. Add zucchini, tomatoes, vegetable stock and seasonings. Cook, uncovered, until zucchini is nearly done, about 10 minutes. Stir in parsley. In bowl, sift together flour, baking soda and baking powder. Stir in cornmeal. Set aside. In mixing bowl beat together egg, 1 tablespoon oil, buttermilk and brown sugar. Add wet ingredients to dry ingredients and mix until moistened. Pour half of vegetables into a greased 8" x 8" baking dish. Spread with polenta mixture. Pour remaining vegetables over the polenta. Bake, at 400 degrees, for 20-25 minutes or until topping is cooked. Add cheese during last 5 minutes of cooking.

Rice Caliente Casserole
Serves 4-6

1 lb. lean ground beef
1 onion, chopped
3-4 large garlic cloves, minced
1 can tomatoes and green chilies
1 cup sour cream
1 cup uncooked rice, prepared according to package directions
salt and pepper to taste
1 lb. mild cheddar cheese, grated

Sauté onion and minced garlic. Add meat. Cook until meat is browned. Remove excess fat. Add tomatoes and green chilies, salt, pepper and rice. Simmer for 30 minutes to 2 hours. Add sour cream and heat thoroughly. Put mixture into a shallow casserole dish. Put the grated cheese on top. Cover. Bake, at 350 degrees, for 45 minutes.

Spinach Soufflé Pie

Serves 6

2 10 oz. packages frozen spinach,
thawed and steamed
1 lb. ground beef or turkey
2 tablespoons horseradish
3 eggs, well beaten
6 oz. mozzarella cheese, grated
1 ready made pie crust

Prepare spinach. Drain excess liquid. Brown meat. Drain excess fat. Combine spinach, meat, horseradish, eggs and cheese. Turn into prepared crust and cover with foil. Bake, at 400 degrees, for 45 minutes. Remove from oven and let set for 5 minutes before serving.

Letty's Garlic Bow Tie Pasta

Serves 4-6

1/2 cup olive oil
8 cloves fresh garlic, minced
1 lb. pasta, bow tie shape
1 cup sun-dried tomatoes, cut
into small pieces
1/8 teaspoon crushed red pepper
1/4 cup minced fresh parsley or basil
(optional)
1 cup lightly steamed broccoli flowerettes
(optional)
1/4 cup toasted pine nuts (optional)
1 cup diced, cooked chicken meat
(optional)
1 cup diced, cooked turkey sausage
(optional)
1/2 cup grated Parmesan cheese
salt and pepper to taste

In medium saucepan, heat olive oil with the garlic over very low heat. Elevate the pan away from the flame in some fashion. The goal is to infuse the garlic flavor into the oil without burning the garlic. This will take about 10 minutes. Meanwhile, cook the pasta in a large pot of boiling salted water until just tender. Drain and set aside. Plump the tomatoes in 1 cup of the hot pasta water for a few minutes. Drain the tomatoes and add them to the garlic oil. Add the pepper and any of the optional ingredients and heat through. Toss in the pasta and the cheese and serve immediately.

DESSERTS

Park City High School Band

*On July 1, 1949 the mines shut down putting
1,200 miners out of work. Park City was listed as
a ghost town in the book "Ghost Towns of the West."
The town was not "deserted" but occupied by
talented young musicians. In 1950, the Park City
High School Band, led by Byron Jones, was chosen
to perform at the Shriner's East-West All-Star
Football game in San Francisco.
Because of Park City's financial hardships, a plea
went out on radio airwaves across the country to
help send the band to California. Within several
weeks $4,000 was raised from Chicago to the West
Coast. The band received a standing ovation for
their performance.*

Chocolate Heath Bar Dessert
Serves 12

1 chocolate cake mix
1/2 cup Kahlua
large box chocolate instant
pudding, prepared
12 oz. Cool Whip, ready to use
4 Heath candy bars, crushed

Prepare cake mix according to package directions. Bake in 9" x 13" pan. Cool 10 minutes. Poke holes with fork 2" apart in cake. Pour 1/2 cup Kahlua over top. Cover with Saran wrap and let sit on counter overnight. Into a large serving bowl, spoon a layer of cake pieces into the bottom of bowl (1/2 the cake), cover layer of cake pieces with layer of pudding, then Cool Whip and half of crushed candy bars. Repeat layers, ending with candy bars on top. Cover with plastic wrap and refrigerate until serving.

The Next Best Thing To...
Serves 12

1 cup unsifted flour
1/2 cup margarine, softened
1 cup chopped pecans
8 oz. cream cheese, softened
1 cup sugar
12 oz. Cool Whip, divided
2 (3.9 oz.) packages instant
chocolate pudding
5.1 oz. package instant vanilla pudding
3 cups cold milk
chocolate shavings

In a medium bowl, mix flour, margarine and nuts until crumbled. Press in the bottom of a 9" x 13" greased pan and bake, at 350 degrees, for 15-20 minutes. Cool. Beat cream cheese and sugar until smooth. Fold in 6 oz. Cool Whip and spread over bottom layer. Combine chocolate and vanilla puddings with milk until smooth and thick. Spread pudding mixture over middle layer. Top with remaining Cool Whip and grate chocolate over top. Refrigerate until serving.

Texas Chocolate Cake
Serves 24

2 cups flour
2 cups sugar
1/4 cup margarine
1/2 cup Crisco
4 tablespoons cocoa
1 cup water
1/4 teaspoon salt
1/2 cup buttermilk
2 eggs
1 teaspoon soda
1 teaspoon cinnamon
1 teaspoon vanilla

Icing:
1/4 cup margarine
4 tablespoon cocoa
6 tablespoons milk
2 cups powdered sugar
1 cup chopped pecans
1 teaspoon vanilla

Mix flour and sugar, set aside. In saucepan, heat margarine, Crisco, cocoa, water and salt. Bring mixture to a rapid boil. Pour over flour and sugar mixture. Stir well. Add buttermilk, eggs, soda, cinnamon and vanilla. Mix well. Pour into a greased 12" x 18" cake pan. Bake 20 minutes at 400 degrees. Start icing 5 minutes before cake is done. In saucepan, melt margarine, cocoa, milk and bring to a boil. Remove from heat. Add powdered sugar, pecans and vanilla. Mix well. Pour over cake while still hot.

English Toffee Bars
Yield: 3 dozen

1 cup butter or margarine
1 cup firmly packed light brown sugar
1 egg yolk
1 teaspoon vanilla
1 cup all purpose flour
5 (1 1/2 oz.) chocolate candy bars
1/2 cup chopped walnuts

Combine softened butter, sugar, egg yolk and vanilla in large bowl mixing with wooden spoon. Stir in flour and mix well. Spread mixture evenly in a greased 15" x 10" x 1" jelly roll pan. Bake, at 375 degrees, for 15 minutes or until top is lightly browned. Break up chocolate over hot toffee layer. Sprinkle evenly with chopped nuts and cut into 2-inch squares.

Perfect Chocolate Cake
Serves 12

1 cup unsifted unsweetened
cocoa powder
2 cups boiling water
2 3/4 cup all purpose flour
2 teaspoons baking soda
2/3 teaspoon baking powder
1/2 teaspoon salt
1 cup butter or margarine, softened
2 1/2 cups sugar
4 large eggs
1 teaspoon vanilla extract

Frosting:
6 oz. semi-sweet chocolate pieces
1/2 cup light cream
1 cup butter or margarine
2 1/2 cup confectioners' sugar

Filling:
1 cup heavy cream
1/4 cup confectioners' sugar
1 1/4 teaspoon vanilla extract

In medium-sized bowl, combine cocoa with boiling water, mixing with wire whisk until smooth. Cool completely. Grease well and lightly flour three round 9" x 1 1/2" cake pans. Sift flour with baking soda, baking powder and salt. Preheat over to 350 degrees. In large bowl of the electric mixer, at high speed, beat butter, sugar, eggs and vanilla until light (about 5 minutes) scraping bowl occasionally. At low speed, beat in flour mixture alternately with cocoa mixture beginning and ending with flour mixture. Divide batter evenly into prepared cake pans. Smooth tops. Bake 25 to 30 minutes or until surface springs back when gently pressed with fingertip. Cool in pans 10 minutes. Carefully loosen sides with spatula. Remove from pans and cool on wire racks. For frosting, combine chocolate pieces, cream and butter in saucepan. Stir over medium heat until smooth. Remove from heat. With whisk, blend in 2 1/2 cups confectioners' sugar. In bowl set over ice, beat until frosting holds its shape. For filling, whip together cream, sugar and vanilla. Assemble cake on plate placing filling between two layers of cake. Frost sides and top with frosting. Refrigerate at least 1 hour before serving.

Pumpkin Cheesecake
Serves 10-12

Crust:
2 1/2 cups graham cracker crumbs
1/2 cup butter, melted
1/2 cup sugar

Filling:
5 eggs
3/4 cup brown sugar
2 1/2 teaspoons vanilla
1/2 teaspoon ginger
1/2 teaspoon nutmeg
1/4 teaspoon cloves
24 oz. cream cheese, room temperature
12 oz. solid pack canned pumpkin
1/2 teaspoon cinnamon

Topping:
16 oz. sour cream
3 tablespoons sugar
1 tablespoon lemon juice
1 teaspoon vanilla

For crust: Mix crumbs, butter and sugar together. Press into bottom and sides of large spring-form pan. Set aside.

For filling: Blend eggs, sugar, vanilla, ginger, nutmeg and cloves at high speed in food processor. Add cream cheese and blend until smooth and all lumps are gone. Add pumpkin and blend until smooth. Pour mixture into prepared crust and sprinkle cinnamon on top. Bake for 60 minutes at 350 degrees (for higher altitude 65-70 minutes) and test for doneness. Cool 5 minutes.

Topping: Gently stir sour cream, sugar and lemon juice until smooth. Pour over top of cooled filling. Return to 350 degree oven for 5 minutes. Cool and refrigerate.

Applecake Finlandia
Serves 16

1 1/2 cups margarine
1 1/3 cup white sugar
3 eggs
2 1/3 cups flour
1 teaspoon baking powder
2 1/2 teaspoons vanilla
apple slices (or peaches or pears)
cinnamon and sugar

Melt margarine and add sugar and eggs, beating slightly. Add flour mixed with baking powder. Finally add vanilla and stir until mixed. Put dough in two greased metal pie plates. Top with apple slices and sprinkle with cinnamon and sugar. Bake 30 minutes at 325 degrees. (Secret: take cakes out of oven when center is still slightly raw.)

Chocolate Caramel Pecan Cheesecake
Serves 10-12

Crust:
2 cups vanilla wafers crumbs
6 tablespoons butter or
margarine, melted

Filling:
14 oz. bag caramels
15 oz. evaporated milk
1 cup chopped pecans
16 oz cream cheese, softened
1/2 cup sugar
2 eggs
1/2 cup semi-sweet chocolate
chips, melted
1 teaspoon vanilla

Heat oven to 350 degrees. For crust, mix wafer crumbs and butter. Press onto bottom and sides of 9-inch springform pan. Bake 10 minutes. Microwave caramels and milk in small microwaveable safe bowl on high for 4-5 minutes or until melted, stirring every minute. Pour over crust. Top with pecans. Beat cream cheese and sugar at medium speed with electric mixer until well blended. Add eggs, one at a time mixing well after each addition. Blend in chocolate and vanilla, pour over pecans. Place pan on cookie sheet. Bake 45 minutes or until done. Loosen cake from rim of pan. Cool before removing rim of pan. Refrigerate. Garnish with whipped cream and additional chopped pecans, if desired.

Strawberry Meringue Pie
Serves 6-8

3 egg whites
1/2 teaspoon baking powder
1 cup sugar
10 (2") squares soda crackers,
rolled fine
1/2 cup chopped pecans
1 quart unsweetened strawberries
1/2 cup heavy cream, whipped

Beat egg whites and baking powder until they form in stiff peaks. Gradually add sugar. Fold in crackers and pecans. Spread mixture into a well buttered 9-inch pie pan. Bake, at 300 degrees, for 30 minutes. Cool. Fill pie crust with sliced strawberries and top with whipped cream. Chill several hours.

Chocolate Applesauce Cake
Serves 16

1 teaspoon cinnamon
2 heaping tablespoons cocoa
1 tablespoon vanilla
dash of salt
2 1/2 cups applesauce
4 cups flour, sifted
3 teaspoons baking soda
2 cups sugar
1 cup shortening
2 eggs

Cream sugar and shortening. Add eggs and beat well. Add cinnamon, cocoa, vanilla, salt and applesauce. Mix well. Add 3 cups of flour a little at a time and stir well. Put soda in the rest of the flour and stir lightly into cake mixture. Place in a greased 10" x 15" x 2" pan. Bake 45 minutes to 1 hour at 350 degrees.

Grandma's Fudge Icing:
2 cups sugar
1/2 cup evaporated milk
1/2 cup light Karo syrup
2 tablespoons butter
1 teaspoon vanilla
1 1/2 to 2 tablespoons cocoa

Combine sugar, milk and Karo syrup in medium sized saucepan. Place 1/2 cup of mixture in bowl and add cocoa, stirring well to eliminate lumps. Add to mixture in saucepan. Cook to soft ball stage. Remove from heat and add butter and vanilla. Stir continuously until mixture thickens. Add small amounts of evaporated milk and continue stirring until mixture can be spread on cake.

Sour Cream Apple Pie
Serves 6-8

pie crust for a 2 crust pie
1 lb. apples, peeled and sliced
(or peaches)
3/4 cup sugar
8 oz. sour cream
5 tablespoons flour
1/4 teaspoon salt
1/4 teaspoon cinnamon
(1/4 teaspoon nutmeg for peaches)

Place bottom crust in pie plate. Place fruit in the bottom of the pie plate. Mix all other ingredients and pour over fruit. Top with whole or lattice crust and sprinkle with cinnamon sugar. Bake at 425 degrees for 15 minutes, then bake at 350 degrees for 45 minutes.

Apple Upside-Down Cake
Serves 8

Topping:
3-4 Golden Delicious apples, peeled
cored and quartered
3/4 cup unsalted butter
2/3 cup sugar
1/2 cup coarsely chopped walnuts

Cake:
1 Golden Delicious apple, peeled
and chopped fine
1 1/2 cup all purpose flour
1 1/2 teaspoon baking powder
3/4 teaspoon salt
1 teaspoon cinnamon
1/2 cup unsalted butter, softened
2/3 cup sugar
1 teaspoon vanilla
2 tablespoons minced fresh ginger root
2 large eggs
1/2 cup sour cream

In a well-seasoned cast-iron 10" skillet, melt butter over moderately low heat just until melted. Stir in sugar until combined well. Arrange apple quarters decoratively, cut sides up, in skillet and sprinkle walnuts evenly in between apples. Cook mixture, undisturbed, 25 to 35 minutes, or until apples are tender in centers and sugar is a golden caramel. Preheat oven to 375 degrees. Make cake while topping is cooking. In a bowl sift together flour, baking powder, salt and cinnamon. In another bowl, with an electric mixer, beat butter and sugar until light and fluffy. Beat in vanilla and ginger root and add eggs, 1 at a time, beating well after each addition. Beat in sour cream and with mixer on low speed beat in flour mixture gradually until just combined. Fold chopped apple into batter. Remove skillet from heat and spoon batter evenly over topping. With a metal spatula spread batter (being careful not to disturb topping), leaving 1/4 inch border of cooked apples uncovered. If using a non-stick skillet with a plastic handle, wrap handle in a double thickness of foil. Put skillet in a shallow baking pan and bake cake in middle of oven 25 to 35 minutes, or until a tester comes out with crumbs adhering and cake is golden brown. Cool cake in skillet on a rack 10 minutes. Run a thin knife around edge of skillet and carefully invert cake onto a plate. Serve cake warm or at room temperature with caramel sauce and whipped cream.

Orange Carrot Cake
Serves 12

2 1/2 cups cake flour
3/4 teaspoon baking powder
3/4 teaspoon baking soda
1 teaspoon salt
1 teaspoon ground cinnamon
3/4 cup vegetable oil
1 egg
1 cup buttermilk
3/4 cup firmly packed light brown sugar
3/4 cup white sugar
2 cups grated carrots (2-3)
2/3 cup chopped walnuts
2 tablespoons finely grated orange rind
1/4 cup orange marmalade

Adjust oven rack to lower third of oven. Preheat oven to 350 degrees. Grease and flour 9" x 2" round cake pan; line bottom with wax paper. Prepare cake. Sift flour, baking powder, baking soda and cinnamon into large bowl. Whisk oil, egg and buttermilk in medium sized bowl to blend. Add brown and white sugars; mix until smooth with no lumps. Stir in carrots, walnuts and orange rind. Add to flour mixture; mix until well blended. Pour into prepared cake pan. (Batter will be thin.) Bake 60 to 65 minutes or until wooden pick inserted in center comes out clean. Cool cake in pan 10 minutes. Run metal spatula around edge of cake. Invert cake onto wire rack. Discard wax paper. Cool completely. Heat orange marmalade in small saucepan until warm and liquid. Brush over top and sides of cake.

Pumpkin Pie Squares
Serves 18

1 package yellow cake mix
1/2 cup melted margarine
1 egg
2/3 cup milk
2 eggs
3 cups canned pumpkin
1/4 cup brown sugar
1 teaspoon cinnamon
1/2 cup margarine

Reserve 1 cup of yellow cake mix. To remaining cake mix, add margarine and 1 egg. Mix well and press evenly into greased 9" x 13" pan. Stir together milk, remaining 2 eggs and canned pumpkin. Spread evenly over bottom layer. For topping, combine reserved cup of cake mix, sugar, cinnamon and margarine. Blend with pastry blender until mixture is crumbly. Sprinkle over filling. Bake, at 350 degrees, for 45 to 50 minutes or until knife comes out clean.

Peach Upside-Down Cake

Serves 12

Topping:
6 tablespoons unsalted butter,
cut into pieces
1/2 cup firmly packed light brown sugar
1 tablespoon dark rum
3 cups sliced, peeled peaches,
patted dry

Cake:
2 1/4 cups all purpose flour
1 tablespoon baking powder
1 teaspoon salt
4 tablespoons unsalted butter, softened
3/4 cup sugar
1 large egg
1 cup milk

Preheat oven to 375 degrees and butter a 10" x 2" round cake pan. Make topping in a small saucepan. Melt butter with brown sugar and rum over moderate heat, stirring occasionally. Spread rum mixture evenly in pan and arrange peach slices on top. Make cake batter. In a bowl sift together flour, baking powder and salt. In another bowl, with an electric mixer, beat together butter and sugar until light and fluffy. Beat in egg until combined. Add half of flour mixture and beat until just combined. Add 1/2 cup milk and beat until just combined. Repeat procedure with remaining flour mixture and milk, ending with flour. Spread batter evenly over peaches and bake in middle of oven until tester comes out clean, about 40 minutes. Immediately invert cake onto a serving plate, leaving pan on top of cake 30 minutes. Carefully remove pan and serve cake warm or at room temperature.

George Washington Cherry Pie

Serves 6-8

Crust:
1 1/3 cup graham cracker crumbs
1/4 cup sugar
1/3 cup butter or margarine, melted

Filling:
3 oz. box cherry gelatin, regular or
sugar-free
20 oz. can cherry pie filling,
regular or "lite"
1 cup boiling water

To make crust, combine cracker crumbs and sugar in a medium bowl and mix well. Add butter and stir. Press crust mixture into 9-inch pie plate and chill in the freezer for about 10 minutes. While crust is chilling, dissolve the gelatin in 1 cup boiling water. When it has completely dissolved, add the canned pie filling. Blend well and pour into the chilled crust. Let set in refrigerator for 1-2 hours until solidified.

Lemon Poppyseed Cake
Serves 8

Fruit Compote:
1/2 cup water
2/3 cup sugar
2 tablespoon fresh lemon juice
1 tablespoon fresh thyme leaves
1 1/4 teaspoon vanilla
4 cups seasonal fruit

Cake:
1 1/4 cup all purpose flour
2/3 cup sugar
1/2 cup cornstarch
2 tablespoons poppyseeds
2 1/4 teaspoons baking powder
1 teaspoon salt
2 tablespoons butter
1 cup skim milk
2 1/4 teaspoons freshly grated lemon zest
1 1/2 teaspoons vanilla
1 egg

In a small saucepan bring water with sugar, lemon juice and thyme to a boil stirring occasionally and boil until sugar is dissolved. Cool syrup to room temperature and stir in vanilla. Combine syrup with fruit. Set aside. Preheat oven to 350 degrees and grease and flour an 8" x 2" cake pan. In a bowl whisk together flour, sugar, cornstarch, poppyseeds, baking powder, and salt and with fingers blend in butter until incorporated. In a large measuring cup lightly beat together milk, zest , vanilla and egg. Stir milk mixture into flour mixture until just blended and pour batter into prepared pan. Bake cake 35 minutes or until tester comes out clean. Remove cake from pan and cool on a rack. Serve wedges of cake topped with fruit compote.

Pineapple Poke Cake
Serves 12

1 yellow cake mix, bake as directed on box
1 large can crushed pineapple
8 oz. cream cheese, softened
1 large instant vanilla pudding
2 cups milk
8 oz. Cool Whip

While cake is hot, poke the cake with a fork in 1/2" intervals. Pour pineapple over the cake. Mix cream cheese with the instant pudding and 2 cups milk. Pour on top of cake. Refrigerate. Cover with Cool Whip before serving.

Picnic Cake
Serves 12

1 cup chopped dates
1 1/2 cups boiling water
1 teaspoon soda
1 cup sugar
3/4 cup shortening
2 eggs
1 1/2 cups plus 2 tablespoons flour
1 teaspoon cinnamon
1/2 teaspoon salt
1 teaspoon vanilla

Topping:
1/2 cup brown sugar
1/2 cup chopped nuts
6 oz. chocolate chips

Pour boiling water over dates and add soda. Cool without stirring. Beat together sugar, shortening and eggs. Add to date mixture. Then add flour, cinnamon, salt and vanilla. Pour into greased and floured 9" x 13" pan. Mix together topping ingredients and sprinkle on top. Bake, at 350 degrees, for 45 minutes.

Pumpkin Roll
Serves 8

Cake:
1 cup sugar
2/3 cups flour
3 eggs
1/2 teaspoon soda
3/4 teaspoon cinnamon
2/3 cup pumpkin
powdered sugar

Filling:
12 oz. cream cheese
3 tablespoon butter
1 teaspoon vanilla
1 cup powdered sugar
1 cup chopped pecans

Stir all cake ingredients together. Pour over greased jelly roll sheet. Bake, at 350 degrees, for 15 minutes. Sprinkle powdered sugar over the cake while hot. While still warm, loosen sides of cake, turn upside down and remove from pan. Mix together filling ingredients. Spread over the cake while still warm. Roll the pumpkin roll lengthwise until a complete roll. Wrap in plastic wrap or foil. Chill 5 to 10 minutes. Slice to serve. Chill any unused pumpkin roll.

Easy Apple Cake
Serves 15

4 cups finely diced apples
2 cups sugar
1/2 cup oil
2 beaten eggs
2 cups flour
2 teaspoons cinnamon
2 teaspoons baking soda
1/2 teaspoon salt
2 teaspoons vanilla
1 cup chopped nuts
powdered sugar

Mix apples and sugar and let stand for 30 minutes. Mix oil, eggs, flour, cinnamon, baking soda, salt and vanilla. Add nuts and apple mixture. Bake, at 350 degrees, for 40 minutes in 9" x 13" pan. Cool and dust with powdered sugar.

Fresh Apple Cake
Serves 12

1 1/2 cup vegetable oil
2 cups sugar
3 eggs
3 cups flour
1 teaspoon baking soda
2 teaspoons cinnamon
1/2 teaspoon nutmeg
1/2 teaspoon salt
3 cups tart apples, peel and diced
1 cup walnuts
2 teaspoon vanilla

Combine and blend oil and sugar. Add one egg at a time. Sift together flour, baking soda, cinnamon, nutmeg and salt. Add to sugar mixture and blend thoroughly. Add chopped apples, walnuts and vanilla. Pour into greased and floured 9" or 10" tube pan. Bake, at 325 degrees, for 1 1/4 hours. Test cake before removing from oven. Let rest in pan. Mix together glaze ingredients. Spoon glaze over cake before removing cake from pan.

Glaze:
2 tablespoons butter, softened
2 tablespoons brown sugar
2 tablespoons white sugar
2 tablespoons heavy cream mixed with
1/4 teaspoon vanilla

Karen's Carrot Cake
Serves 18

2 cups flour
2 teaspoons cinnamon
2 teaspoons baking soda
4 eggs
2 cups sugar
1 1/2 cup oil
2 cups shredded carrots
1 cup chopped walnuts
7 oz. coconut

Frosting:
8 oz. cream cheese, softened
1/2 cup margarine
1/2 teaspoon vanilla
3 3/4 cups powdered sugar

Sift together flour, cinnamon and soda. Mix in all other ingredients. Bake in greased and floured 9" x 13" pan, at 350 degrees, for 45 minutes. Cream together frosting ingredients. Spread evenly over cooled cake.

Strawberry Trifle
Serves 16

1 yellow cake mix
5 oz. box Danish dessert, strawberry flavored
4 oz. box vanilla pudding mix
10 oz. package frozen strawberries, thawed
1 pint whipping cream, whipped (or Dream Whip)

Make the yellow cake mix according to package directions. When cool, break into bite sized pieces. Make Danish dessert according to package directions. Cool. Make pudding according to package directions. Cool. Add berries to Danish Dessert. In glass bowl, layer cake with Danish Dessert and pudding. Top with whipped cream.

Pumpkin Spice Cake
Serves 12-16

2 cups flour
2 teaspoons soda
1/2 teaspoon salt
1 teaspoon ground cloves
2 teaspoons cinnamon
1 teaspoon ginger
2 cups sugar
1 cup salad oil
4 eggs
29 oz. can pumpkin
1 cup raisins
1 cup walnuts

Frosting:
8 oz. cream cheese, softened
1 tablespoon butter
1 teaspoon vanilla
3 3/4 cups powdered sugar

Sift together dry ingredients. Set aside. In mixing bowl combine sugar and oil. Add eggs. Add pumpkin. Add dry ingredients. Fold in raisins and walnuts. Bake in a greased 9" x 13" pan for 50 minutes at 350 degrees. Mix together frosting ingredients and spread evenly over cool cake.

Marble Bundt Cake
Serves 12

2 cups sugar
1 cup margarine
3 eggs
1 cup milk or orange juice
1 1/2 teaspoons vanilla
2 teaspoons baking powder
3 cups flour
1/4 cup chocolate syrup
1/2 teaspoon baking soda

Mix together sugar and margarine. Beat eggs in one at a time. Add milk. Add vanilla, baking powder and flour. Mix until smooth. Add 2/3 of the batter to a greased and floured bundt pan. Add chocolate and baking soda to the remaining batter and mix. Add to the bundt pan and make a design by cutting in with a knife. Bake, at 350 degrees, for 65 minutes.

Vanessa's Grandma's Lemon Pound Cake
Serves 10

1 cup butter
1 tablespoon Crisco
1 2/3 cup sugar
5 eggs
3 1/2 cups flour
3 teaspoon baking powder
1 teaspoon salt
1 cup milk
1 teaspoon vanilla
2 teaspoons lemon juice

Glaze:
1/3 cup lemon juice
2/3 cup sugar
3 tablespoons butter

Cream together butter, Crisco and sugar. Add eggs one at a time. Sift together flour, baking powder, salt and add alternately with milk. Add vanilla and lemon juice. Beat until well mixed. Pour into a greased and floured tube pan. Bake, at 325 degrees, for one hour or until done. Cool. Heat glaze ingredients in saucepan over low heat. Spoon glaze over cooled cake.

Pears Renee
Serves 6-8

6 slightly underripe pears, halved, cored and peeled
3/4 cup dry white wine
1/3 cup orange juice
1/4 cup brown sugar
1 teaspoon cinnamon (scant)
1 quart vanilla ice cream, slightly thawed
1/2 small can of orange juice concentrate

Cook first 5 ingredients in a covered skillet for 8 minutes. Uncover and cook 20 minutes more. Cool slightly. Serve with orange ice cream. (To make orange ice cream, mix together orange juice concentrate and slightly thawed vanilla ice cream. Refreeze until serving time.)

Macadamia Pound Cake
Serves 12

Cake:
2 cups sweetened flaked coconut
(about 6 oz.)
1 1/2 cup macadamia nuts
1 cup unsalted butter, softened
1 2/3 cups firmly packed light
brown sugar
8 oz. cream cheese, softened
4 large eggs
1 1/2 tablespoons vanilla
2 2/3 cups all purpose flour
2 1/2 teaspoons baking powder
1 teaspoon salt

Glaze:
1/4 cup water
3/4 cup sugar
1/3 cup dark rum

Preheat oven to 350 degrees and butter and flour a 10-inch bundt pan. Spread coconut in a shallow baking pan and toast in middle of oven, stirring occasionally and watching carefully to avoid burning, until golden, 10 to 12 minutes. Transfer coconut to a bowl and cool. Spread nuts in pan and toast in middles of oven until pale golden, 8 to 10 minutes. Cool nuts and chop coarsely. In a bowl with an electric mixer, beat together butter and brown sugar until light and fluffy and beat in cream cheese. Add eggs, 1 at a time, beating well after each addition and beat in vanilla. Sift flour, baking powder and salt into bowl and beat just until combined well. Stir in coconut and chopped nuts. Spread batter evenly in pan and bake in middle of oven 1 hour to 1 hour and 10 minutes, or until tester comes out clean. Cool cake in pan for 5 minutes and then invert onto rack. Make glaze by bringing water and sugar to a boil, stirring until the sugar is dissolved. Stir in rum. Brush hot glaze evenly over outside of warm cake until absorbed. Cool cake completely.

Fresh Blackberry Pie
Serves 8

2 pie crusts
2 1/2 pints fresh blackberries
1 tablespoon freshly squeezed
lemon juice
1 cup sugar
1/4 cup all purpose flour
1/3 teaspoon ground cinnamon
1/8 teaspoon ground nutmeg
2 tablespoons butter or margarine
1 tablespoon milk
1 tablespoon sugar for topping

Line 9-inch pie plate with pie crust. Preheat oven to 400 degrees. Sprinkle blackberries with lemon juice. Mix together 1 cup sugar, flour, cinnamon and nutmeg. Sprinkle over blackberries. Place blackberry mix in prepared pie crust. Dot with butter. Cover berries with top crust. Cut a 2-inch cross in center of pie. Fold back each corner to make a steam vent. Crimp out edges of crust together in a decorative fashion. Brush top with milk and sprinkle with 1 tablespoon sugar. Place strips of foil around edge of pie to prevent crust from overbrowning. Bake 40 to 45 minutes or until juices bubble through steam vent and crust is golden brown. Cool at least one hour before serving.

Fresh Lime Pie
Serves 8

1 pie crust
4 large egg yolks
14 oz. can sweetened condensed milk
1 1/2 teaspoon grated lime zest
1/2 cup fresh lime juice
few drops green food coloring (optional)
1 cup chilled heavy cream
2 tablespoons confectioners' sugar
4 lime slices, twisted
fresh raspberries (garnish)

Bake pie crust 8 to 10 minutes; cool. In a medium-sized bowl, beat egg yolks with electric beater for about 5 minutes or until thick and lemon colored. Add condensed milk, lime zest, lime juice and food coloring; beat until smooth. Turn into baked pie crust, spreading evenly. Refrigerate pie several hours or overnight. Before serving, beat cream and confectioners' sugar together until mixture forms stiff peaks. Spread over pie and garnish with lime slices and fresh raspberries.

Mandelbrot
Yield: 1 1/2-2 dozen bars

1/2 cup sugar
3 eggs
1/2 cup corn oil
1 teaspoon vanilla
1 teaspoon almond extract
1 cup chocolate chips
1 cups pecans or almonds
3 cups flour
2 teaspoons baking powder

Beat together sugar and eggs until creamy. Mix in oil, vanilla and almond extracts. Add chocolate chips. Finely chop nuts in food processor and add to batter. Mix flour and baking powder in separate bowl, then add to batter. Make ball with dough and cut in half. Stretch out each half and flatten out on cookie sheet into wide 1/2-inch flat ovals. Bake, at 350 degrees, until light brown (about 15 minutes). Slice diagonally into 3/4-inch slices and turn on sides. Bake until medium brown (about 10 minutes). Cool. (Similar to biscotti but not as hard or as sweet.)

Chocolate Layer Bars
Yield: 3 dozen

2 cups semisweet chocolate chips
8 oz. cream cheese
2/3 cups evaporated milk
1 cup chopped walnuts
1 teaspoon almond extract, divided
3 cups flour
1 1/2 cups sugar
1 teaspoon baking powder
1/2 teaspoon salt
1 cup butter, softened
2 eggs

Combine chocolate chips, cream cheese and evaporated milk in saucepan. Cook over low heat, stirring constantly until chips are melted and mixture is smooth. Remove from heat, stir in walnuts and 1/2 teaspoon almond extract. Blend well, set aside. Combine remaining ingredients in large mixing bowl. Blend well until mixture resembles coarse crumbs. Press half of mixture in greased 9" x 13" pan. Spread chocolate mixture on top. Sprinkle rest of crumbs over filling. Bake, at 375 degrees, for 35 to 40 minutes or until lightly golden brown. Cool. Cut into bars.

Oatmeal Cookies
Yield: 3 dozen

1 cup all purpose flour
1/2 cup white sugar
1/2 cup packed brown sugar
1/2 teaspoon salt
1/2 teaspoon baking soda
1/2 cup shortening
1 egg
2 tablespoons milk
1 teaspoon vanilla
1 1/2 cup quick-cooking oats
1 cup raisins

In large mixing bowl stir together the flour, sugars, salt and soda. Add the shortening, egg, milk and vanilla. Stir with wooden spoon until well mixed or mix with your hands. Mix in oats and the raisins. Preheat oven to 350 degrees. Drop dough by teaspoonfuls onto greased cookie sheets, about 2 inches apart. Bake for 12 minutes.

Chocolate Chip Cookies
Yield: 3-4 dozen

3/4 cup sugar
3/4 cup brown sugar
1 cup butter
2 eggs
1 teaspoon vanilla
2 1/4 cup flour
1 teaspoon baking soda
1 teaspoon salt
2 cups chocolate chips

Melt butter and add sugars. Mix well and add eggs and vanilla. Mix well. Add flour, baking soda, salt and mix completely. Blend in the chocolate chips. Drop by teaspoonful onto ungreased baking sheet. Bake, at 350 degrees, for 7 to 10 minutes or until lightly browned.

Chocolate Peanut Butter Balls

Yield: 8 dozen

2 cups margarine or butter
18 oz. crunchy peanut butter
3 1/2 cups powdered sugar
3 1/4 cup Rice Krispies
1 teaspoon vanilla
24 oz. semi-sweet or milk
chocolate chips

Mix first five ingredients with hands and form into small bite-sized balls. Refrigerate overnight. Melt chocolate chips in double boiler. Dunk peanut butter ball in chocolate and set on wax paper. Refrigerate.

Miniature Peanut Butter Treats

Yield: 3-4 dozen

1/2 cup Crisco
1/2 cup brown sugar
1/2 cup white sugar
1 egg
1/2 cup creamy peanut butter
1/2 teaspoon vanilla
1 1/4 cup flour
3/4 teaspoon baking soda
1/2 teaspoon salt
miniature peanut butter cups

Cream together Crisco, sugars, egg, peanut butter and vanilla. Add flour, baking soda and salt; beat until smooth. Cover and chill. When cool enough to handle easily, roll into small (walnut-sized) balls. Place each ball in greased miniature muffin tin. Bake, at 375 degrees, for 8 to 9 minutes. Remove from oven. Gently press 1 peanut butter cup into each cookie. Cool in pan for 10 minutes; remove carefully from tins and cool on rack.

Peppermint Creams
Yield: 4 dozen

1/2 cup whipping cream
1 lb. 6 oz. imported white chocolate,
finely chopped
1 cup finely crushed hard peppermint
candies (about 7 oz.)
1/2 teaspoon peppermint extract
6 oz. semi-sweet or milk chocolate chips
48 small candy paper cups

Spread paper cups onto cookie sheet. Bring cream to a simmer in medium saucepan. Remove from heat. Add white chocolate and stir until melted. Whisk in crushed peppermint candies and peppermint extract. Spoon quickly into paper cups. Press down with wet fingers to smooth tops. Melt chocolate pieces over hot water. Spread on top of mint candies. Add a little crushed peppermint on top if desired.

Oatmeal Chocolate Chip Cookies
Yield: 3 dozen

2 cups chocolate chips, divided
1 1/2 cup oatmeal
1 cup butter
1 cup white sugar
1 cup brown sugar
2 eggs
1 teaspoons vanilla
1 3/4 cups flour
1 teaspoon baking soda
1/2 teaspoon salt
1 1/2 cups chopped nuts

Preheat oven to 375 degrees. In food processor, combine 1/2 cup chips and 1 1/2 cup oats for about 15 seconds. Cream butter and sugars first. Add eggs and vanilla. In a separate bowl mix flour, baking soda, salt and chocolate and oat mixture. Gradually add dry ingredients to wet ingredients. After dough is fully mixed, stir in chocolate chips and walnuts. Drop onto cookie sheet in rounded teaspoons about 1-inch apart. Bake 8-10 minutes.

Caramel Chocolate Squares
Yield: 2 1/2 dozen

1 cup all purpose flour
1/2 cup firmly packed brown sugar
1/3 cup butter or margarine, softened
5 chocolate coated caramel and
marshmallow bars, cut up
1/4 cup milk
2 eggs, lightly beaten
1 teaspoon vanilla
2 tablespoons all purpose flour
1/2 teaspoon baking powder
4 oz. blanched, sliced almonds

Combine flour and sugar in a small bowl. Cut in butter until ingredients form a crumbly dough. Press mixture into a greased 9" x 13" pan. Bake, at 350 degrees, for 12 minutes or until light golden. Cool in pan on wire rack while preparing filling. Melt candy bar with milk in a small saucepan over moderately low heat. Cool slightly then very slowly beat into eggs in a small bowl, beating constantly to prevent curdling. Beat in vanilla, then flour mixed with baking powder. Pour filling over crust. Sprinkle almonds over top. Bake, at 325 degrees, for 25 minutes or until top is firm. Cool in pan. Cut into squares or bars.

Peanut Butter Cookies
Yield: 3 dozen

1 cup shortening
1 cup peanut butter
1 cup white sugar
1 cup packed brown sugar
2 eggs
1 teaspoon vanilla
2 1/4 cups all-purpose flour
2 teaspoons baking soda
1/4 teaspoon salt

In large bowl, mix shortening and peanut butter with wooden spoon. Add both kinds of sugar. Stir until mixed. Stir in eggs and vanilla until mixed. In medium bowl stir together flour, soda and salt. Stir into sugar mixture until well mixed. Use your hands to mix the dough, if you need to. Preheat oven to 350 degrees. Form dough into balls. Put on ungreased cookie sheets. Flatten with a fork. Bake for 10 to 12 minutes.

Applesauce Spice Cookies
Yield: 2 dozen

1/2 teaspoon baking soda
1/2 cup applesauce
1/2 cup margarine, softened
1 cup sugar
1 egg
2 cups flour
1/2 teaspoon cloves
1/2 teaspoon cinnamon
1/2 teaspoon nutmeg
1/2 teaspoon salt
1/2 cup chopped nuts, optional

Add baking soda to applesauce and let set for 15 minutes. Cream margarine and sugar together. Add egg. Mix flour with spices and salt. Add to creamed mixture. Add applesauce (and nuts, if desired). Drop by spoonfuls on greased cookie sheet. Bake, at 350 degrees, for 15 minutes. Frost cookies, if desired, with powdered sugar icing.

Icing: 1 cup powdered sugar mixed with 1-2 tablespoons milk

Baked Apples
Serves 5

5 cooking apples (such as Granny Smith, Macintosh or Pippin)
2/3 cup cranberries
2/3 cup chopped walnuts
1/2 cup brown sugar
1/2 cup bread crumbs
1 teaspoon cinnamon
zest of 1 lemon
5 tablespoons unsalted butter

Preheat oven to 375 degrees. Wash and core apples, then remove one-half inch from the bottom of each so they sit flat in the roaster. Combine remaining ingredients. Stuff each apple with filling, generously mounding on top. Bake for approximately 25 minutes until filling is cooked and bubbly. Serve hot or cold.

New England Pudding
Serves 6

1/4 cup corn meal
3 cups milk
3/4 cups molasses
1/3 cup firmly packed light brown sugar
1/4 cup butter or margarine
3/4 teaspoon ground cinnamon
1/2 teaspoon ground ginger
1/4 teaspoon salt
1/2 cup seedless raisins
whipped cream (optional garnish)

Mix corn meal and 1 cup of the milk in a small bowl. Heat 2 cups of the milk in the top of a double boiler over hot, but not boiling, water until steaming. Stir in corn meal mixture and cook 15 minutes, stirring occasionally. Stir in molasses and brown sugar; cook 2 minutes. Remove from heat; stir in butter, cinnamon, ginger, salt and raisins, mixing well. Spoon into a buttered 1-quart casserole. Add remaining milk. Bake, at 325 degrees, for 1 1/2 hours or until knife inserted in center comes out clean. Top with whipping cream, if desired.

Park City Peach Cobbler
Serves 8

Filling:
1/2 cup water
1/2 cup brown sugar
2 tablespoons cornstarch
2 16 oz. packages frozen peach slices,
thawed and drained
1 tablespoon fresh lemon juice

Topping:
1 cup flour
1/2 cup sugar
1 1/2 teaspoons baking powder
1/2 teaspoon salt
1/4 cup butter, softened
1/2 cup milk
1/2 teaspoon grated nutmeg

Prepare filling by combining water, brown sugar, cornstarch in a saucepan over medium heat. Bring to boil stirring constantly until thickened. Remove from heat, stir in peaches and lemon juice. Pour into 1 1/2-quart baking dish. Prepare topping by combining flour, sugar, baking powder, salt and butter with pastry blender until it resembles coarse crumbs. Stir in milk until well blended. Spoon dough over peach filling and sprinkle with nutmeg. Bake, at 350 degrees, for 30 to 35 minutes until lightly browned. .

Honey Orange and Almond Tagliatelle
Serves 4-6

1/2 lb. dried egg tagliatelle
dash of sunflower oil
4 oranges
5 tablespoons clear honey
3 tablespoons light brown sugar
1 tablespoon lemon juice
3 tablespoon butter
2/3 cup flaked almonds

Bring a large pan of water to a boil and add the tagliatelle with a dash of sunflower oil. Cook for 10 minutes until tender. Drain and set aside. Peel and slice three of the oranges. Squeeze juice from the remaining orange into small saucepan. Add honey, sugar and lemon juice. Bring to a boil and simmer for 1 to 2 minutes until syrupy. Melt the butter in a large frying pan. Fry the flaked almonds until golden. Stir in the tagliatelle and honey syrup, heat through, then quickly stir in the orange slices. Serve immediately.

Flan
Serves 8

3/4 cup sugar
3 eggs
3 egg yolks
2 teaspoons vanilla
1 can sweetened condensed milk
1 3/4 cup milk
2 oz. cream cheese

Stir sugar over medium heat until liquid is deep golden brown. Pour into bottom of pie plate. Place remaining ingredients into blender and blend 3 to 5 minutes. Pour over sugar in pie plate. Place pie plate in pan. Pour boiling water 1/2 way up side of dish. Bake, at 350 degrees, for 70 minutes or until set.

Fresh Fruit Tart
Serves 8

Dough:
3/4 cup butter, softened
1/4 cup confectioners' sugar
1 1/2 cup all purpose flour

Filling:
2/3 cup blanched almonds
1/2 cup sugar, divided
6 tablespoons unsalted butter,
room temperature
1 large egg and 1 egg yolk,
beaten together
1 tablespoon Kirsh or strawberry liqueur
2 tablespoons all purpose flour

Topping:
1/2 cup strawberry jelly
fresh fruit

Dough: Cream together 3/4 cup butter and 1/4 cup sugar in food processor. Add flour until coarse and grainy. Place in a plastic bag and refrigerate for 30 minutes. Press the dough into the bottom and sides of a 10-inch tart pan.

Filling: Grind almonds with 2 tablespoons sugar in food processor. Set aside. In mixer, blend butter and remaining sugar. Add egg, egg yolk and Kirsh. Next, add the flour and almond sugar mixture. Spread in unbaked tart shell. Bake, in bottom of oven, at 425 degrees, for 10 minutes. Lower temperature to 350 degrees and bake for 10 to 12 minutes or until golden. Remove and cool on rack.

Topping: Heat strawberry jelly until melted. Brush half of melted jelly over top of tart. Cut strawberries in half and layer around entire tart. Continue with strawberries and desired fruits. Brush fruit with remaining jelly.

Russian Cream with Raspberry Sauce
Serves 4-8

3/4 cup sugar
1 envelope unflavored gelatin
1/2 cup water
1 cup whipping cream
1 1/2 cup sour cream
1 teaspoon vanilla
mint sprig (garnish)

Raspberry sauce:
10 oz. package of frozen raspberries, thawed
1 teaspoon almond extract

In a medium-size saucepan, blend the sugar and gelatin. Add water and mix well. Let stand for five minutes, stirring occasionally. Bring to a full boil, remove from heat and let stand until cool. In the meantime, mix the creams and vanilla in a large pitcher. When the gelatin mixture is cool enough to touch, but not so cold as to have gelled, pour it through a fine sieve into the pitcher of cream. Blend with a long whisk and pour into serving dishes. Let chill at least 4 hours or as long as overnight. Make raspberry sauce by forcing thawed raspberries through sieve to strain out seeds. Add 1 teaspoon almond extract. Pour a thin layer on top of set cream. Garnish with a sprig of mint.

Cranberry Casserole
Serves 8

1 bag cranberries
3 cups chopped apples
1 cup sugar
1 cup quick-cooking oatmeal
1/2 cup brown sugar
1/2 cup walnuts or pecans, chopped
4 tablespoons butter or margarine

Mix cranberries, apples and sugar together in a small mixing bowl, then put into a baking dish. In a separate bowl mix oatmeal, brown sugar and nuts. Spread on top of cranberry mix. Cut 4 tablespoons of margarine or butter into pats and scatter on top of oatmeal. Bake, uncovered, for 1 hour at 325 degrees.

French Apple Crepe with Burnt Almond Cream
Serves 8

Crepes:
3/4 cup milk and water
3 large eggs
1 tablespoon sugar
3 tablespoons orange liqueur,
rum or orange juice
1 cup all purpose flour
5 tablespoons melted butter

Burnt Almond Cream:
1/2 cup sugar
6 tablespoons butter, room temperature
2 large eggs
1 1/3 cup sliced almonds, toasted
1/2 teaspoon pure almond extract
1/2 teaspoon pure vanilla extract
3 tablespoons dark rum

Apple Filling:
12 large apples
juice of 1 to 2 lemons
sugar, to taste

Mix crepe ingredients in blender. Heat an 8-inch non stick pan and spray with a non stick spray (such as Pam). Pour about 1/4 cup of the crepe mixture in the pan and cook until the top of crepe looks almost done. Turn and cook 30 seconds longer. Remove from pan and stack on a plate. Beat all burnt almond cream ingredients together in bowl. If made ahead, stir over warm water to keep spreadable. Peel and core the apples. Slice into 1/4-inch thick slices. Put apples in a large pan and toss with lemon juice and sugar. Cook until tender. To assemble dessert, lay a crepe on the bottom of a 9-inch springform pan and top with some of the apples. Spoon a few tablespoonfuls of the burnt almond cream over the apples. Top with another crepe and press down to flatten the crepe. Continue to repeat steps of layering until you finish with apples on top. Bake, in a preheated 375 degree oven, for about 30 minutes until bubbling hot and apples on top are nicely browned. Serve hot or at room temperature.

Caramels
Yield: 9 dozen

1 cup butter
2 1/4 cup brown sugar
dash of salt
1 cup Karo light syrup
1 can Eagle Brand condensed milk
1 tablespoon vanilla

Melt butter, sugar and salt together. Very, very slowly add the Karo and condensed milk. Cook until hard ball stage (about 15 minutes). Pour into 9" x 13" buttered pan. Cool. Cut and wrap in waxed paper.

Dixie Peanut Brittle
Yield: 2 1/2 lbs.

2 cups sugar
1 cup light corn syrup
1/2 cup water
1/2 teaspoon salt
4 cups raw shelled peanuts, skin on
2 tablespoons butter
2 teaspoons baking soda

In heavy saucepan, heat sugar, syrup, water and salt to a rolling boil. Add peanuts. Reduce heat to medium and stir constantly. Cook until syrup spins a thread (290 degrees). Add butter, then baking soda. Beat rapidly and pour on a buttered surface (heat pan first), spreading to 1/4-inch thickness. When cool break into pieces.

Carla's World Famous Caramel Sauce
Yield: 4 cups

2 cups brown sugar
1 cup light Karo syrup
1/2 cup butter, room temperature
1 1/3 cups sweetened condensed milk

Mix sugar and Karo. Bring slowly to a boil while sugar is dissolving. Then boil 3 minutes. Add butter and boil for 1 minute. Add sweetened condensed milk and boil for 3 minutes. Great over ice cream or pound cake. Cook a little longer - about 5 minutes, then pour over hot popped corn. It has to be eaten within a few hours and makes a great, gooey caramel corn.

HISTORICAL

Park City Union Pacific Depot

*Utah Eastern Railroad was the first to complete its
line from Coalville into Park City in December
1880. Three years later, the railroad was taken
over by Union Pacific, who built the depot at the
bottom of Main Street in 1886. Many Chinese
railroad laborers helped build the railroads and
joined the Cornish, German, Scottish, Irish and
Scandinavian miners in making Park City their
home. Each nationality brought with them their
expertise and national character. The Cornishmen,
often referred to as "Cousin Jacks", created new
terms for food such as: "stirabout"- oatmeal mush
diluted with milk and "Cornish pasties"-thin meat
turnovers. The Cornish pasty became "a letter from
home" when a miner's wife tucked one into her
husband's lunch bucket.*

*The recipes in this section have been passed down from generation to generation.
We have published the recipes exactly as we have received them.*

Pickled Vegetables

1 pint whole small cucumbers
1 pint sliced cucumbers
1 pint whole small onions
1 cup string beans
3 sweet green peppers, sliced
3 sweet red peppers, sliced
1 pint tomatoes or cauliflower flowerettes

Dressing:
1 quart vinegar
4 tablespoons flour
1 cup brown sugar
3 tablespoons dry mustard
1 tablespoon celery seed
1/2 tablespoon turmeric
1/2 cup vinegar
1/2 cup water

Fill pint jars with vegetables. Heat dressing to 180 degrees. Do not boil. Pour hot dressing over vegetables to within 1/2-inch of the top of the jar. Seal and process in hot water bath for 15 minutes.

Beef and Apple Stew
Serves 8

1 cup dried apples
3 lb. round steak, cut in pieces
1 cup celery
hot water or stock
salt and pepper to taste
1 onion, minced
shreds of lemon rind
mashed potatoes

Soak overnight 1 cup of dried apples. Brown meat in an iron kettle containing melted fat. Add 1 cup diced celery and the apples. Cover with hot water or stock. Season with salt, pepper, onion and a few shreds of lemon rind. Cover and simmer gently until the meat is tender. Thicken the liquid, around the stew, with a little flour smoothed in cold water. Serve in the center of a platter surrounded by a border of mashed potatoes.

Miners' Cornish Pasties
Serves 5

Crust:
1 1/4 cup shortening
3 cups flour
1/3 cup cold water
1 egg, beaten
1 tablespoon vinegar

Filling:
1 lb. round steak, in 3/8" cubes
2 potatoes
1 small onion, finely chopped
1 teaspoon parsley, chopped
2 teaspoons salt
1/2 teaspoon pepper
2 tablespoons butter

Cut shortening into flour until small beads appear. Stir in water, egg and vinegar. Roll into a ball. Refrigerate until chilled. Roll out. Using an 8" plate as a guide, cut out 5 circles. Set aside. Combine steak, potatoes, onion and parsley. Sprinkle with salt and pepper. Toss. Put a mound of filling in center of each circle. Dot with butter. Fold half of circle over mound. Press edges. Cut slits in top. Put in baking dish. Bake at 400 degrees for 20 minutes. Reduce heat to 325 degrees. Bake 45 more minutes. To keep hot, wrap in aluminum foil and put in paper bag.

Cornish pasties came from England with the wives of emigrating miners. They were carried underground in the miners lunch boxes, wrapped in newspaper to keep them warm and reheated in a shovel held over a candle at lunch or dinner time.

Dandelion Salad
Serves 4

1 lb. dandelion greens
other vegetables as desired
2 strips crisp, fried bacon, crumbled

Dressing:
1/4 cup vinegar
1 tablespoon brown sugar
1 tablespoon bacon drippings

Gather tender leaves of the dandelion before flowers appear (to avoid bitter taste). Rinse in cold running water. Tear into bite-sized pieces for salad and mix with garden vegetables or wild onions. Combine dressing ingredients and add to salad. Toss and serve.

Fish Pickle

6-8 or 1 lb. whole, small fish or
pieces of large one
2 tablespoons oil
1/2 cup water
1/2 cup vinegar
2 tablespoons minced onion
1 teaspoon mixed pickling spice
or bay leaf
1/2 green or red pepper,
seeded and diced
1 teaspoon salt
1/8 teaspoon pepper

Gently simmer fish in salted water until cooked, or use leftover fried fish. Mix remaining ingredients in a mixture. Cover and let stand in refrigerator at least 24 hours, turning fish occasionally. Serve cold as a relish, or as a main dish.

Fruit Cake
Serves 8

1 cup of brown sugar
large cup of molasses
1 teaspoon each: cinnamon, allspice,
nutmeg and cloves
6 eggs, beaten
1 1/2 cups of coffee
3 oz. of brandy
2 quarts of flour
1 teaspoon of soda
1 lb. of citron and lemon peel
1/2 lb. of butter
2 lb. currants
2 lb. of raisins

Bake slowly 2 hours at 300 degrees.

Cabbage Chowder
Serves 4

1 small head cabbage, chopped
1 medium onion, chopped
1 tablespoon fat
3-4 cups cubed ham
1 lb. bulk sausage (or links)
1/2 teaspoon salt
1/8 teaspoon pepper
dash of cayenne
2 tablespoons flour
2 cups milk
1 cup rice, cooked

Melt fat. Add sausage and cubed ham and stir well until browning begins. Add the cabbage and onions. Stir well. Water can be added to prevent burning. Add salt, pepper and cayenne. Cover and simmer until cooked thoroughly. Blend the flour with enough milk to make it smooth; add it and the remainder of the milk to the chowder and cook about five minutes more. Serve over steamed rice.

Doughnuts
Mrs. McNicholas
Yield: 1 1/2 dozen

4 cups flour
2 cups sugar
2 teaspoons baking powder
2 teaspoons salt
2 teaspoons nutmeg
2 eggs, beaten
2 tablespoons lard
pint of buttermilk
1 teaspoon of soda

Mix ingredients together. Knead lightly 6 times. Pat or roll dough to 1/2-inch thick. Cut into biscuits, using 2 1/2-inch biscuit cutter. Fry, in preheated grease, for 1 1/2 minutes or until golden. Drain. Sprinkle with sugar.

Ginger Pudding
Serves 8

1 teaspoon soda
1 cup sour milk
2 cups butter
1 cup sugar
5 eggs, well beaten
1 cup molasses
4 cups flour
ginger and allspice to taste

Combine soda and milk. Let stand 10 minutes. Beat butter while adding sugar slowly. Beat in eggs, one at a time. Add molasses. Mix and sift flour, ginger and allspice. Add to egg mixture alternately with milk mixture. Turn into greased baking dish; cover. Bake, in 350 degree oven, for 1 1/4 hours.

Sauce:
half pint of molasses
1 pint of sugar
1/2 pint butter
ginger to taste
a little water

Boil all ingredients together until sauce is thick.

Black Cake
Serves 12

1 lb. sugar
3/4 lb. butter
12 eggs
2 lb. currants and raisins
1/2 lb. citron
teaspoon each of nutmeg and cloves
2 glasses of wine
2 glasses of brandy
small cup of molasses
6 eggs
one cup of strong coffee
soda, if you like

Mix well. Bake, at 350 degrees, 35-40 minutes.

Farmer's Fruit Cake

Serves 12

3 cups dried apples
2 cups molasses
2 eggs
1 cup sugar
1 cup sweet milk
3/4 cup butter
1 1/2 teaspoons soda
enough flour to make a stiff batter
spices, to taste

Soak three cups of dried apples overnight in warm water, chop slightly in the morning, then simmer two hours in two cups of molasses until the apples resemble citron. Make a cake of two eggs, one cup of sugar, one cup of sweet milk, three quarters of a cup of butter, one and a half teaspoonfuls of soda and flour enough to make a stiff batter. Spice well and add the apples last. Bake in quick oven.

Dried Apple Cake

Serves 12

2 cups dried apples
1 cup sugar
1 cup sour milk
2 eggs
heaping teaspoonful of soda
spice to taste
a few raisins or currant
flour to make a stiff batter

Two cups of home dried apples, the quarters cut in two. Let them simmer all day on back of stove; then let stand overnight to cool. Add one cup sugar, one cup sour milk, two eggs, heaping teaspoonful soda, spice to taste, a few raisins or currants, flour to make a stiff batter. Bake like any fruit cake. This will make two loaves.

Golden Yolk Cake
Serves 12

12 egg yolks
1 3/4 cups sugar
1 cup, plus 3 tablespoons boiling milk
2 1/4 cups flour
1 3/4 teaspoons baking powder
1/4 teaspoon vanilla

Beat yolks until thick and very light. Add sugar gradually, beating continuously until very light. Add hot milk gradually and mix until blended. Sift flour, baking powder and salt together several times and add gradually to the above mixture. Beat until smooth. Bake in a 350 degree oven for 30 minutes for layers, 45 minutes or longer for a tube cake.

Sourdough Starter I

1 cup warm water
1 1/4 cup white flour
1 teaspoon salt
1 teaspoon sugar
1 medium sized raw potato, grated

Place mixture in wide mouth jar and mix well. Cover with cheesecloth for 24 hours. With loose lid, let stand to ferment for 2 weeks. Or, mix 1 cup warm water, 1 cup flour and 1 tablespoon sugar. Let stand for several days, until full of bubbles.

Sourdough Starter II

1 cup buttermilk
1 cup flour

Mix well and let stand at least 48 hours or until it starts to ferment and has a pleasing sour odor. Each time the starter needs to be replenished, add flour and evaporated milk in equal amounts, allowing crock to stand in warm place at least 12 hours - cover tightly and store in refrigerator until needed.

Thin Sourdough Pancakes

Serves 4-6

2 cups basic batter
1 egg
2 tablespoons cooking oil
1 cup evaporated milk
1 teaspoon salt
1 teaspoon baking soda
2 tablespoons sugar

Combine basic batter, egg, cooking oil and evaporated milk and beat thoroughly. Combine salt, soda, sugar and blend together until smooth, eliminating any lumps of soda. Sprinkle evenly over the top of batter and fold in evenly. This will cause a gently foaming, rising action. Allow batter to rest a few minutes and fry on a hot, lightly greased griddle. If batter seems too thick, thin with a little milk or water.

Sour Dough Waffles

Serves 4-6

1/2 cup starter
1 cup milk
1 cup warm water
1 3/4 cups flour
2 eggs
1 tablespoon sugar
1/2 teaspoon salt
1 teaspoon baking soda
4 tablespoons oil

Combine starter, milk, water and flour in a large bowl. Mix to blend and leave at room temperature overnight. Next morning add, egg, sugar, salt, soda, oil and mix well. Bake in a hot waffle iron until well browned.

Miners Biscuits
Yield: 15 biscuits

1 large egg, beaten lightly
2/3 cup milk
2 cups all-purpose flour
1 tablespoon sugar
1/2 teaspoon sugar
2 teaspoons baking powder
1/2 cup lard
vegetable oil

Preheat oven to 450 degrees. In a bowl whisk together egg and milk. Into another bowl sift together flour, sugar, salt and baking powder. Blend in lard with a pastry blended or fingertips until mixture is fine and crumbly. With a fork, stir egg mixture into flour mixture until just combined. Dough will be moist. On a well-floured work surface, knead dough gently several times until it comes together and is smooth. Pat dough into a 3/4" thick circle about 7-inches in diameter. Cut dough into rounds with a small glass or 2-inch biscuit cutter. Lightly press scraps together and continue cutting biscuits in same manner. Roll each biscuit in oil, letting excess drip off and arrange on a large baking sheet about 2 inches apart. Bake biscuits in middle of oven for 10 minutes. Reduce temperature to 400 degrees and bake biscuits 8 to 10 minutes more or until golden brown.

Cornish Splits
(Soft White Rolls)
Yield: 22

1/4 cup lukewarm water
3/4 cup milk
1 teaspoon sugar
two 1/4 oz. packages active dry yeast
(5 teaspoons)
3 cups all-purpose flour
1 teaspoon salt
1/4 cup cold lard, cut into pieces

In small saucepan heat water with milk just until lukewarm and remove pan from heat. Stir in sugar and yeast and let stand until foamy, about 5 minutes. While yeast is proofing, in a bowl whisk together flour and salt and with a pastry blender, or fingertips, blend in lard until mixture resembles coarse meal. Add milk mixture to flour mixture and stir until a dough forms. On a lightly floured surface, knead dough gently just until smooth, about 1 minute. Transfer dough to a lightly oiled large bowl and turn to coat with oil. Let dough rise, bowl covered, in a warm place until doubled in bulk, about 45 minutes. Grease two baking sheets. Punch down dough and divide into 1 1/2-inch balls. Transfer balls to baking sheets and let rise, covered loosely, in a warm place until doubled in bulk, about 30 minutes. Preheat oven to 375 degrees. Bake splits in upper and lower thirds of oven, switching position of sheets halfway through baking, 20 minutes, or until golden. Serve splits hot or at room temperature.

Prize Recipe Contest
San Francisco Examiner
Serves 4

1 chicken
6 tablespoons butter, divided
1 onion slice
2 cups boiling water
1 cup canned corn
1 cup canned tomatoes
1 cup lima beans
4 small potatoes
flour
salt and pepper, to taste

Disjoint chicken, brown a sliced onion in three level tablespoons of butter and put the chicken in to brown lightly. Pour in two cups of boiling water and set back to cook slowly until nearly tender. Skim well and put in a cup of canned corn, a cup of canned tomatoes and a cup of canned lima beans. Cook half an hour, then add four small potatoes that have been sliced and cooked in the boiling water five minutes. Thicken with three level tablespoons of butter rubbed smooth with the same amount of flour and season with salt and pepper.

Grated Fresh Potato Cakes
Serves 4

4 average-size new potatoes, grated
1 small winter onion, grated
large green pepper, chopped
3 eggs, slightly beaten
bacon fat

Combine ingredients, except bacon fat. Form into patties. Fry in hot bacon drippings, at least 1/4 inch deep, in skillet.

Potato Dumplings
Serves 4

2 cups grated potatoes
1 1/2 cups flour
meat broth or other liquid

Mix potatoes and flour. Roll into balls. Drop into hot meat broth or other liquid. Cook until done.

French-Fried Onion Rings
Serves 6-8

1 1/2 cups flour
1/2 teaspoon salt
2/3 cup milk
1/2 cup cream or evaporated milk
3 tablespoons salad oil
2 egg whites, unbeaten
5-6 medium onions

Sift flour and salt into mixing bowl. Add milk, cream, oil, egg whites and beat until smooth. Cut peeled onions into 1/4 inch slices and separate into rings. Dip each ring into batter and drip a few at a time into oil heated to 365-375 degrees. Fry about three minutes. Drain on absorbent paper towel, sprinkle with salt.

Dandelion Wine
Yield: 4 gallons

4 gallons boiling water
3 gallons dandelion blooms
1 1/2 quarts orange juice
1 pint lemon juice
8-10 lb. sugar
1 package dry yeast

Pour 4 gallons boiling water over dandelion blooms. Let stand 30-36 hours. Strain thoroughly, pressing out all juice. In large (6-10 gallon) container, place dandelions, orange juice and lemon juice. Add sugar and stir until dissolved. Sprinkle package of dry yeast over top, cover with towel and let stand in warm place for 6 weeks. Siphon off dregs. Let stand to clear 1 month, then bottle. This is better if you can let it stand a year before drinking.

Home Made Soap

7 lb. clean grease
2 1/2 gallons water
2 cans lye
4 oz. borax
1 cup ammonia

blossoms, to scent

To be made outside in a 5 gallon container. Bring to a boil 7 pounds of clean grease and 2 1/2 gallons of water. Slowly add 2 cans of lye then 4 ounces of borax. Let boil until it is the consistency of honey. Add one cup of household ammonia. Then fill the container to within one inch of the top with boiling water. Let stand for 2 to 4 days. Then turn out, cut in sections and store. For scented soap, take part of the last addition of water and boil rose petals, geranium leaves, lilac blossoms, or the like. Strain and add to the mixture. Makes a lovely soap. Not hard on the skin!

Tooth Powder

1 tablespoon salt
3/4 tablespoon soda
1 teaspoon finest precipitated chalk
(get at drug store)
few drops of oil of wintergreen
for flavoring

Horse Colic

1 pint aniseed oil
1 oz. ether
2 oz. Laudanum mix

CHILDREN

Schoolmates

Park City has a long history of fine schools for
its children. In 1875, the Ontario Mine opened
Park City's first school for its miners' children.
In 1879, the Park City Free School was established
and was soon followed by St. Mary's Catholic
School, the New West School and the Park City
Academy. The George Washington, the Jefferson,
the Lincoln and finally the Marsac followed. Only
the buildings for the Washington and the Marsac
remain today and house a small inn and the
municipal offices respectively. By 1887, there were
500 students attending these schools. Today,
there are over 3,000 students in the Park City
School District. Education continues to be an
important part of Park City.

Emmy's Graduation Punch

Serves 16-24

4 cups cranberry juice cocktail
10 packages Equal
4 cups pineapple juice
1 tablespoon almond extract
2 quarts ginger ale

Create premix with first four ingredients. Just before serving, combine premix and ginger ale.

Homemade Root Beer

Yield: 2 liters

7 cups distilled or purified water
1 1/2 cups white sugar
1/4 teaspoon active dry yeast
1 teaspoon of root beer concentrate

Microwave water on high setting for three minutes (or heat the water on a cooktop until lukewarm). Add the sugar, yeast and root beer concentrate to the water and stir slowly until sugar and yeast dissolve. Fill a 2-liter bottle, leaving 2 inches of air space at the top. Screw on the bottle cap tightly to assure proper carbonation. Lay the bottle on its side in a warm place and leave it undisturbed for four days. On the fifth day, put the root beer in the refrigerator to chill. It will be ready to drink on the sixth day. If the flavor is too strong, add a small amount of cold water.

Love Potion

Serves 2

1/2 cup frozen strawberries,
slightly thawed
1/2 cup frozen raspberries,
slightly thawed
1 cup white grape juice (or apple juice)
strawberry (garnish)

Place first three ingredients in a blender on high until you have a uniform color. Garnish with stawberries.

Peek-A-Boo Eggs
Serves 1

1 slice of bread, white or whole wheat
1 egg
2 teaspoons butter or margarine

With a cookie cutter, cut 2 to 3 inch design in the slice of bread. Melt butter in a small skillet over medium heat. Drop bread in the pan and crack the egg into the hole in the bread. Cook for approximately 2 minutes. Flip the bread and let the egg cook 2 minutes more. Toast the bread cut out and spread with peanut butter and jelly.

Domino Treats

graham crackers
cream cheese
peanut butter
chocolate chips, butterscotch chips or white chocolate chips

Spread each graham cracker piece with cream cheese or peanut butter. Arrange chips in a domino pattern.

Frozen Orange French Toast
Serves 6

2 eggs
1 cup orange juice
1 tablespoon sugar
1/4 teaspoon salt
12 slices French bread
6 tablespoons butter or margarine.

Beat together first four ingredients. Dip bread into egg mixture, coating both sides. Place bread on baking sheets and freeze until firm. Wrap securely and return to freezer. Before serving, place frozen bread slices in well-buttered, shallow baking dish. Melt butter and drizzle over bread. Bake in preheated, 500 degree oven, for 5 minutes. Turn bread and bake 5 minutes more. Dust with powdered sugar and serve with syrup.

Egg Boats
Yield: 12 boats

6 eggs
2 tablespoons mayonnaise
dash of salt and pepper
colorful construction paper
12 toothpicks or straws

Hard boil the eggs. Cook and cut eggs in half. Remove the egg yolk. In a medium bowl combine the mayonnaise, salt, pepper and egg yolks until creamy. While the eggs are cooking cut out paper triangles, about 2 inches high, for sails. Tape the triangles to the toothpicks. Spoon egg mixture into halved egg whites and position sails in the middle of the "boat".

Pretzel Snacks
Yield: 15

1 package yeast
1 1/2 cup warm water
1 teaspoon salt
1 tablespoon sugar
4-5 cups flour
1 egg, beaten

Dissolve yeast in warm water. Combine salt, sugar and 4 cups of flour in a large bowl. Mix ingredients together and knead dough on a floured surface. Shape dough into pretzels, letters, shapes or numbers. Place shapes on a lightly greased cookie sheet. Brush the dough shapes with the beaten egg. Bake, at 425 degrees, for 12 minutes. Cool slightly and serve.

Macaroni and Cheese
Serves 8

1 lb. macaroni, cooked slightly less than directions
1 lb. grated mild cheese

White Sauce:
1/2 cup butter
2 tablespoons flour
2 1/2 cups milk
salt and pepper to taste

To make the white sauce: In medium saucepan, melt butter. Blend in the flour. Gradually add the milk and cook over low to medium heat until mixture thickens. In a large casserole, layer half of the macaroni with half of the cheese. Repeat. Pour the white sauce over the top. Cover. Bake at 300 degrees for 1 1/4 hour or until done.

Tuna Pita Sandwich
Serves 4

1 can white or light tuna, drained
1 medium onion, chopped
3/4 cup celery, chopped
1/4 teaspoon garlic
1/2 cup mayonnaise
16 slices cucumbers
lettuce or sprouts
salt and pepper to taste
4 whole wheat pita breads

Mix tuna, chopped onion, chopped celery, garlic and mayonnaise. Cut pita breads in half and lightly toast in toaster. Put 3 tablespoons tuna mixture into each half. Add 2 slices of cucumber and a piece of lettuce or sprouts to each pita. Salt and pepper to taste.

Saturday Night Special
Serves 4-6

1 lb. extra lean ground beef
1 onion, chopped
1 can chicken gumbo soup
2 tablespoons catsup
2 tablespoons mustard
salt and pepper to taste

Brown meat and onions. Add remaining ingredients. Simmer, covered for 30 minutes. Serve over hamburger buns or toasted English muffins.

Festive Tuna Sandwich
Serves 8

1 cup yellow cheese, grated
3 hard-cooked eggs, cubed
1 cup flaked white albacore tuna
2 teaspoons celery
1 teaspoon onion, chopped
2 teaspoons sweet pickle, diced
1/2 cup mayonnaise
dash of salt
8 hamburger buns

In a large bowl mix first 8 ingredients in the order given. Fill buns and serve as a cold sandwich or wrap in aluminum foil and heat, at 300 degrees, for 5 to 10 minutes.

Chicken Nuggets
Serves 3-4

2/3 cup ketchup
2 tablespoons honey
2 tablespoons prepared
spicy-brown mustard
1 lb. boneless chicken breasts cut
into 1-inch cubes
1/2 cup corn meal
1 tablespoon melted butter
1/4 cup flour
1/2 teaspoon chili powder

Heat oven to 350 degrees. Grease baking sheet. Blend ketchup, honey and mustard. Remove 1/2 cup of the sauce mix for dipping. Place chicken in sauce and toss. Combine cornmeal and butter. Stir in flour and chili powder. Add chicken and toss until coated. Bake 15 to 18 minutes. Serve with dipping sauce.

Spaghetti Pie
Serves 6

6 oz. spaghetti
2 tablespoons margarine
1/2 cup Parmesan cheese
2 eggs, slightly beaten
1 lb. ground beef
1/2 cup onion
1/4 cup green pepper
8 oz. tomatoes
6 oz. tomato paste
1 teaspoon sugar
1 teaspoon oregano
1/2 teaspoon garlic salt
1 to 1 1/2 cups ricotta cheese or
cottage cheese
1 cup Mozzarella cheese, shredded

Cook spaghetti according to package directions. Drain. Stir in margarine, eggs and Parmesan cheese. In a 10-inch pie plate, form a crust with the noodle mixture. Brown beef, onion and green pepper. Drain. Stir in tomatoes, tomato paste and seasonings. Spread ricotta or cottage cheese over crust. Top with meat mixture. Bake, uncovered at 350 degrees, for 30 minutes. Sprinkle with Mozzarella cheese and bake 5 minutes more.

Marsha's Royal Icing

For Graham Cracker Houses
Yield: 2 cups

2 teaspoons egg whites
3 cups confectioners' sugar
1/4 teaspoon cream of tartar

Using an electric mixer; beat the egg whites with 1 cup sugar and the cream of tartar until well blended. Add the remaining sugar 1 cup at a time. Continue mixing until creamy and smooth. Spoon half of mixture into a ziploc bag with a small hole cut in one corner. Reserve rest of the frosting for spreading on large surfaces.

Ice Luminaria

a one-gallon ice cream bucket
a little vegetable oil
a small votive candle

Rub a little vegetable oil all over the inside of the ice cream pail. Fill the pail with water and put it where the temperature is freezing - outside or in your freezer. After 4-5 hours the water should be partially frozen. Scoop out a hole in the middle and place your candle inside. Let the ice continue freezing until hard. Just before using, take the ice block out of the bucket and light the candle. For added effect, use food coloring to shade the water.

Snow Ice Cream

3 cups loose clean snow
2 tablespoons milk
1/4 cup sugar
1 teaspoon vanilla extract.

Mix all ingredients. Sweeten or flavor to taste.

Homemade Finger Paint
Yield: 4 cups

1 cup all-purpose flour
4 cups cold water, divided
food coloring

In a large saucepan combine 1 cup all-purpose flour and 1 cup cold water. Stir until smooth. Add 3 cups additional cold water. Cook and stir over medium heat until mixture thickens and bubbles. Reduce heat and pour into three heat-proof bowls. Use food coloring to tint desired colors. Cover with plastic wrap and let stand at room temperature until cool. Spoon paint on paper and design with your fingers!

Squeeze Paint
Yield: 2 cups

1 cup flour
1/4 cup salt
1/4 cup sugar
3/4 cup water
4 recycled squeeze bottles
food coloring

Mix flour, salt. sugar and water. Divide into bottles. Add different food coloring to each bottle. Put tops on tightly. Squeeze paint to create a design on construction paper. paint will dry like thick glue. For holiday pictures, add glitter to the mixture.

Glob
Yield: 1 cup

4 oz. white school glue
1 cup water, divided
liquid food coloring
1 teaspoon Borax

Pour the glue and 1/2 cup water into a bowl. Mix. Add a few drops of food coloring. Put remaining 1/2 cup water in another bowl. Add Borax and mix well. Pour two mixtures together and stir. You should have a thick mass in a liquid. When the glob has formed into one chunk, pour off the remaining liquid. The mixture thickens when you knead, stretch and play with it.

Silly Stuff
Yield: 2 cups

2 cups liquid starch
1 cup white glue

Stir liquid starch and glue until a ball forms. Mix with your hands until excess liquid drains off. If mixture is too sticky, add more starch. Store in a plastic bag in the refrigerator. Use Silly Stuff to duplicate your favorite comic strip characters. Just flatten the putty out on top of the newspaper comic strip and peel off. Re-knead and try again.

Peanut Butter Dough

2 cups peanut butter
2 cups powdered milk
3 tablespoons honey

Combine ingredients in a medium bowl. If too sticky, add more powdered milk, one tablespoon at a time. If desired, add chopped nuts or raisins.

No-Cook Dough

2 teaspoons cooking oil
1 cup salt
1 1/4 cup water
2 tablespoons cornstarch
3 cups all-purpose flour

In a large bowl, combine all ingredients. Knead until smooth. Divide dough into equal parts and add food coloring. Add small amounts of water if dough is dry, or flour if dough is sticky.

Cooked Clay

food coloring
2/3 cup water
2 cups salt
1 cup cornstarch
1/2 cup water

Add food coloring to 2/3 cup water. Mix salt and colored water in a saucepan and stir over low heat for aproximately 4 minutes. Remove from heat. Add cornstarch and remaining 1/2 cup water. Stir until smooth. When cool, break into clumps and sculpture your clay.

TESTERS & CONTRIBUTORS

TESTERS

Peg Anderson
Kerby Avedovech
JoAnn Boraas
Kim Carson
Carla Coonradt
Lori Darr
Jo Duthie
Joette Hessick
Cindy Smith
Connie Sutterfield
Leslie Swisher
Betty and Bill Thompson
Lisa Weisman
Kathy Wood
Dana Zimmerman
Nancy Beaufait
Alyson Brighton
Patricia Constable
Corrine Crandall
Mary Demkowitz
Luann Flanders
Penney Hamilton
Dale Hart
Pam Hart
Shauna Hood
Marcia Larcher
Juanita Marshall
Kim Meehan
Sue Morgan
Carole Sanders
Zizi Schirf
Carol Sletta
Ann Sturgis
Suzie Talkington
Joan Townsend
Jane Washington
Betty Watts
Jan Watts
Priscilla Watts

RECIPE CONTRIBUTORS

Joan Alvey
Kristine Anderson
Peg Anderson
Kerby Avedovech
Gerrie Barnett
Dee Beck
Carol Beil
Carolyn Brauer
Barbara Breen
Kathleen Britton
Sharron Brockman
Kim Carson
Janie Chudleigh
Margery Clark
Kathy Clements
Patricia Constable
Carla Coonradt
Kelly Coonradt
Al Cooper
Sidney Creer
Julie Crittenden
Carol Dalton
Linda Dolán
Chad Dougherty
Sheridan England
Don Fielder
Dottie Fielder
Edna Fisher
Letty Flatt
Barbara Fontaine
Cheryl Fox
Bill Geisdorf
Deborah Goldberg
Pam Hart
Mike Hessick
Shaunna Hood
Apolonia Hopkins
Judie Howatt
Ursula Hummel
Sharron Jones
Lou Ann Birkbeck Jorgensen
Randee Kadziel
Barbara Kemp

Brenda Lake
Nancy Langford
Linda Martin
Mary McEntire
Julie McTavish
Kym Meehan
Helena Merrill
Gail Milligan
Kathy Moore
Paula Moore
Andrea Nass
Peggy Nelson
Claire Perrier
Jackie Piland
Sydney Reed
Barbara Roberts
Carmen Rogers
Tami Sacks
Nancy Samson
Carole Sanders
Ted Scheffler
Nancy Scott
Sara Shand
Kathy Shoulders
Linda Singer
Dale Smetana-Nelson
Cindy Smith
Hal Smith
Lynette Spriggs
Holly Stava
Kitty Stothart
Connie Sutterfield
Kimberlee Tafoya
Michelle Taylor
Diana Thompson
Joan Townsend
Laurie von de Ahe
Jane Washington
Priscilla Watts
Suze Weir
Lorri Wolff
Teresa Woodard
Donna Woolsey

INDEX

INDEX

INDEX

INDEX

INDEX

INDEX

INDEX

INDEX

PARK CITY

EDUCATION FOUNDATION

Park City A Taste of Past & Present
Park City Education Foundation
P.O. Box 681422
Park City, UT 84068

To order additional cookbooks contact the Park City Education Foundation at (801) 645-5600 ext. 135

ORDER FORM

Please send *Park City A Taste of Past & Present* to:

Name: _____

Address: _____

City: _____

State: _____ Zip: _____

Telephone No.: (_____) _____

Price	Quantity		Total
$19.95	_____		$_____

Please make checks payable to the
Park City Education Foundation or charge
to VISA or Mastercard.

Acct.#: _____

Expiration Date: _____

Signature: _____

*Profits from the sale of this cookbook are used by the
Park City Education Foundation to support the
Park City schools.*

Shipping & handling
$3.50 per book $_____

Total enclosed $_____

Park City A Taste of Past & Present
Park City Education Foundation
P.O. Box 681422
Park City, UT 84068
(801) 645-5600 ext. 135

- -

ORDER FORM

Please send *Park City A Taste of Past & Present* to:

Name: _____

Address: _____

City: _____

State: _____ Zip: _____

Telephone No.: (_____) _____

Price	Quantity		Total
$19.95	_____		$_____

Please make checks payable to the
Park City Education Foundation or charge
to VISA or Mastercard.

Acct.#: _____

Expiration Date: _____

Signature: _____

*Profits from the sale of this cookbook are used by the
Park City Education Foundation to support the
Park City schools.*

Shipping & handling
$3.50 per book $_____

Total enclosed $_____

Park City A Taste of Past & Present
Park City Education Foundation
P.O. Box 681422
Park City, UT 84068
(801) 645-5600 ext. 135

ORDER FORM

Please send *Park City A Taste of Past & Present* to:

Name: _____

Address: _____

City: _____

State: _____ Zip: _____

Telephone No.: (_____) _____

Price	Quantity	Total
$19.95	_____	$_____

Please make checks payable to the
Park City Education Foundation or charge
to VISA or Mastercard.

Shipping & handling
$3.50 per book $_____

Acct.#: _____

Total enclosed $_____

Expiration Date: _____

Signature: _____

Park City A Taste of Past & Present
Park City Education Foundation
P.O. Box 681422
Park City, UT 84068
(801) 645-5600 ext. 135

Profits from the sale of this cookbook are used by the
Park City Education Foundation to support the
Park City schools.

- -

ORDER FORM

Please send *Park City A Taste of Past & Present* to:

Name: _____

Address: _____

City: _____

State: _____ Zip: _____

Telephone No.: (_____) _____

Price	Quantity	Total
$19.95	_____	$_____

Please make checks payable to the
Park City Education Foundation or charge
to VISA or Mastercard.

Shipping & handling
$3.50 per book $_____

Acct.#: _____

Total enclosed $_____

Expiration Date: _____

Signature: _____

Park City A Taste of Past & Present
Park City Education Foundation
P.O. Box 681422
Park City, UT 84068
(801) 645-5600 ext. 135

Profits from the sale of this cookbook are used by the
Park City Education Foundation to support the
Park City schools.